The Little Book of

CRICKET
LEGENDS

RALPH**DELLOR** and STEPHEN**LAMB**

The Little Book of

CRICKET
L E G E N D S

This edition first published in the UK in 2006
By Green Umbrella

© Green Umbrella Publishing 2006

www.greenumbrella.co.uk

Publishers Jules Gammond, Tim Exell, Vanessa Gardner

Printed and bound in China

ISBN 1-905009-51-8

CONTENTS

CONTENTS

SYDNEY**BARNES**

Born: Smethwick, Staffordshire, 19th April 1873
Died: Chadsmoor, Staffordshire, 26th December 1967
Test Debut: Australia v England, Sydney 1901
27 Tests, 189 wickets at 16.43
Best Bowling: 9/103 v South Africa, Johannesburg 1913

It is never easy to compare players of one generation with those of another. In most cases it is simply enough to say they were the best of their time. That is undoubtedly true with **Sydney Barnes**, for to a man batsmen who faced him said they had never encountered a more searching examination of their skills. Such was his mastery of the art that it is entirely justifiable to claim that he was the greatest bowler who ever lived.

Consider the evidence for that challenging statement. In all types of cricket he took 6,229 wickets at 8.33 each. For a variety of reasons he played in only 27 Test matches, yet he took 189 wickets at 16.43 apiece. All his caps came against Australia and South Africa – the leading batting sides of the time – while only ten of his Tests were played at home. Against Australia alone, he took 106 wickets at 21.58. In 133 first-class matches, he took 719 wickets at no more than 17.09 apiece.

The question has to be asked why he played so little first-class and Test cricket if he was such a force in the game. The answer is simple. He had an obstinate streak and was never an easy character with whom to deal. He played when he felt like it, and most of his long career – he was still bowling when over 60 – was spent playing in the leagues and for Staffordshire, where he was comfortable and could command a larger income than playing county cricket.

So what type of bowler was he? He could move it through the air both ways, and late at that. He could bowl both varieties of cutter and spin it both ways. Quite simply, he was the most complete bowler the game has seen and he was equally adept in whatever style he adopted to suit the prevailing conditions. When asked why he did not bowl a googly, he replied: "I didn't need one."

He had an easy, rhythmical approach to the wicket, transferring the ball from left to right hand just before going into an upright action with a high arm. He was

BELOW

The England team that toured Australia in 1911/12: (back row, l-r) Bert Strudwick, Sep Kinneir, Tiger Smith, Frank Woolley, Jim Iremonger, Phil Mead, 'Young' Jack Hearne, Bill Hitch, Joseph Vine; (front row, l-r) Sydney Barnes, Wilfred Rhodes, Johnny Douglas, Pelham Warner, Frank Foster, Jack Hobbs, George Gunn.

blessed with large hands and developed a vice-like strength in his long, sinuous fingers. In fact, he claimed that he did not swing the ball in a conventional manner when the shine went, as it did early in his day with no manicured outfields and not even a new ball to be taken in mid-innings until 1907. Instead, he could impart such spin on the ball, even when bowling at pace, that it would swerve in the air.

It was the game's good fortune that Barnes ever played the limited amount of first-class cricket he did. It was even more fortuitous that he appeared in Test cricket at all, although there were a host of batsmen who would have disagreed with that statement.

He made his first-class debut in 1894, appearing in four matches for Warwickshire. He then went into the leagues in Lancashire where he began his phenomenal success.

Lancashire invited him to play in two matches in 1899, and two more in 1901 when he began to take serious wickets. Even so, he had only 13 victims to his name when, while appearing for his club, Burnley, play was halted as a telegram was delivered to Barnes. It was from Archie MacLaren who had experienced the difficulties of facing the great bowler in the Old Trafford nets. With total disregard for convention, it was an invitation to tour Australia the following winter.

Barnes began his Test career with a five-wicket return, and claimed another victim in the second innings before claiming 13 more in the second Test.

He limped out of the next encounter with a knee injury, the result of too much bowling. Back home the following summer, he was given just one Test against Australia, before disappearing from Test cricket until 1907. By than he had disappeared from first-class county cricket as well. He had fallen out with Lancashire in 1903 and from 1904 he plied his trade with Staffordshire for 30 years.

On the 1907/08 Australian tour he took 24 wickets. He played against Australia in three Tests at home in 1909 (17 wickets) before returning Down Under in 1911/12 to take 34 wickets in five Tests. He did not prosper at home against Australia in the 1912 triangular series, but he did against South Africa with 34 wickets, at 8.29, in three Tests. He bettered that on the mat in South Africa in 1913/14, when he was virtually unplayable. Four Tests produced 49 wickets costing 10.93 each, including 17 for 109 in the second Test in Johannesburg – the best match haul for any bowler until Laker worked his magic at Old Trafford in 1956.

Barnes was 40 years of age at the time and while that was the end of his Test career, he appeared in a handful of first-class matches thereafter and was still playing league cricket into his sixties. In all, he took 3,741 wickets at a cost, if that is the right word, of 6.83 in the leagues, while his final season of 1934, when he was 61, saw his wickets come at under 11 apiece. However greatness is measured, Barnes can be counted amongst the greatest of them all.

LEFT
Sydney Barnes demonstrates his bowling action, 1920.

FAR LEFT
Sydney Barnes of Warwickshire, Lancashire, Staffordshire and England, 1910.

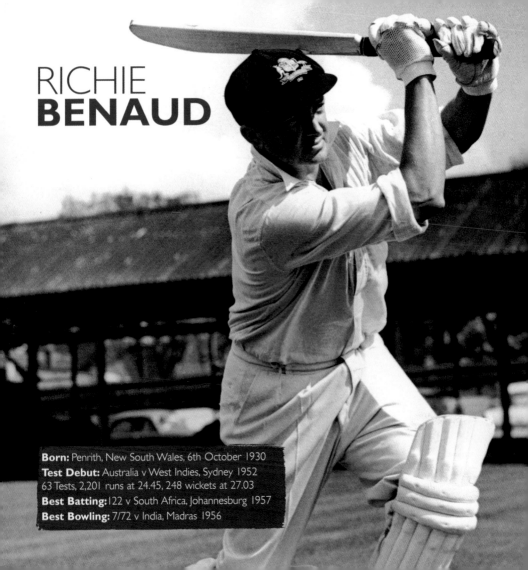

RICHIE
BENAUD

Born: Penrith, New South Wales, 6th October 1930
Test Debut: Australia v West Indies, Sydney 1952
63 Tests, 2,201 runs at 24.45, 248 wickets at 27.03
Best Batting: 122 v South Africa, Johannesburg 1957
Best Bowling: 7/72 v India, Madras 1956

There are a number of disciplines of the game in which Richie Benaud could be described as a legend. As a leg-spinning all-rounder he set new standards, as a captain he was reckoned to be one of the shrewdest of them all, while as a commentator he was peerless. He simply oozed cricket knowledge from every pore without ever being overbearing.

It says something for the modern, television age that whatever his achievements as a player, it was as a commentator that he was best known. He was not one of those players who made his way straight off the field thinking the media owed him a living. Benaud had trained as a journalist before reaching the heights as a player, and so found it relatively easy to combine a thorough understanding of the game with an ability to express himself.

Whether he was employed to deliver his thoughts in print or on the air, he always maintained the highest professional standards. He spent many years commuting between Australia and England to follow the sun as a television commentator. It was said that he never once forgot where he was by, for example, talking about "sundries" in England nor giving the score as " 284 for seven" when in Australia. Much imitated but never emulated, his commentaries remained fresh, keen and totally relevant right up to the moment when he completed his final stint in the UK at the end of the 2005 Ashes series.

Benaud came from a cricketing family. His brother, John, also played for Australia, while the boys' father was a good enough grade cricketer in Sydney to have once taken all 20 wickets in a match. Even so, Richie appreciated that pedigree counted for nothing unless inherent gifts were nurtured. He made himself into a top cricketer by dint of hours of practice, absorbing knowledge and then applying it with a finely-tuned cricketing brain.

He was 18 when he made his debut for New South Wales, and he made his first

appearance in a Test at the age of 21 in the final match of the 1951/52 series against the West Indies in Sydney. He missed the first Test against South Africa the following season, but appeared in the remaining matches as a prelude to his first tour of England in 1953.

It was in South Africa in 1957/58 that Benaud came to the fore as a world-class all-rounder with 106 wickets (30 of them in the five Tests) and 817 runs with four hundreds. It was an opportune time to rise through the ranks, for when Ian Craig's illness forced him to miss the next series, at home to England, Benaud was elevated to the captaincy. Australia regained the Ashes and he remained in the post until 1963.

Benaud was never at his best in England. He made three tours but, not a great spinner of the ball and relying more on bounce to get his wickets, he found that English pitches were not of the type he would want to roll up and carry around with him. Nonetheless, it was at Old Trafford in 1961 that he made history with a remarkable spell of bowling.

England were cruising towards a comfortable victory in the fourth Test. 150 for one chasing 256 suggested that the hosts were set for a two-one lead in the series. Despite severe pain in his bowling shoulder, Benaud took the ball himself and bowled round the wicket into the rough caused mainly by the extensive follow-through of Fred Trueman. Had the English batsmen not been chasing the result, they might simply have padded Benaud away. As it was, they saw this as an opportunity to finish the match with a flourish.

150 for one became 163 for five as Benaud dismissed Ted Dexter, Brian Close, Peter May and Raman Subba Row in five overs. He then accounted for John Murray and David Allen to finish with six for 70 from 32 overs as England were bowled out for 201. In doing so, he made the Ashes safe for Australia once again.

After the success against England, Benaud took the Australian side on victorious tours of Pakistan and India, and set the tone with Frank Worrell for the series against the West Indies in 1960/61 which included the tied Test in Brisbane before Australia's series win. He again retained the Ashes when England went to Australia in 1962/63.

As those results would suggest, he was an inspiring captain who brought the best out of his players as individuals and as a team. He was thoughtful and innovative, while all the time displaying a tough, competitive streak. Able to turn the game himself with an outstanding spell of bowling, a forceful innings, a blinding gully catch or an intelligent piece of captaincy, Benaud had a great array of weapons in his armoury and the intelligence to use them effectively. A genuine legendary cricketer.

ALLAN
BORDER

Born: Cremorne, Sydney, New South Wales, 27th July 1955
Test Debut: Australia v England, Melbourne 1978
156 Tests, 11,174 runs, average 50.56
Best Batting: 205 v New Zealand, Adelaide 1987

When Kim Hughes resigned from the Test captaincy at a tearful press conference in 1984, Australian cricket was at a low ebb. Still suffering from Packer defections, the team was unable to match the powerful sides from around the world that were preying on its obvious weaknesses. Hughes had been a fine stroke maker but was not necessarily a strong, uncompromising leader. Border offered everything that Hughes lacked.

BELOW
Allan Border celebrates in Christchurch, New Zealand, after going to the top of the all-time Test run-scoring list in 1993.

He was more of a pugnacious left-handed batsman than a player to excite the aesthetic senses (John Woodcock wrote that he had "not so much a style as a modus operandi"), but he could chisel out innings of significant magnitude. He was a scrapper, as tough as teak, and no battle was ever lost while Border was involved. From a trough of despair, he dragged, coerced and when necessary bullied Australian cricket into a position from which his players could become undisputed world champions. By the time he had finished with it, the national side was playing in his image.

Border's monumental success did not just happen. He learned his trade playing grade cricket in Sydney and league cricket in Lancashire. He never stinted when it came to practice. When he travelled to play for Essex in 1986, he arrived in Chelmsford after the long and tiring flight from Australia, took his wife and young family to the house that had been secured for them, before going to the County Ground for a net.

He made his debut for New South Wales in 1977 against Tasmania, in a match where he made more of an impression with his left-arm spin than as a batsman. Nought, batting at number seven, and eight not out did not hint at what was to come. But he did feature in a winning side on his debut, just as he would for Australia.

His Test debut came in the Boxing Day match against Mike Brearley's England in 1978. Border managed 29 in the first innings and was run out for nought in the second, but it was Australia's only win in

the series. In the next Test, in Sydney, he scored 60 and 45, undefeated in both innings, to ensure that while a succession of players came and went during the years of World Series Cricket, the name of AR Border would appear again and again on Australian scorecards.

His maiden Test century came later in the year against Pakistan, and by the time he had shown all his grit and fortitude on a tour of India, he was established as Australia's number three. The West Indian pace battery found a weakness outside his off stump, but he recorded the first of his eight Test centuries against England and rounded off a busy and successful season with magnificent innings of 150 not out and 153 against Pakistan in Lahore. It was the first time anyone had scored 150 in both innings of a Test.

Border went over the border in domestic terms at the end of the 1979/80 season, leaving New South Wales for the very good reason that his new wife, Jane, came from Queensland. Eventually he played in the state's first Sheffield Shield winning side but following the move, his form was uncertain more or less right through to the 1981 tour of England. He finished that series on the losing side, but not before he had made two hundreds in the final two matches, despite a

broken finger, and closed with an average of 59.22.

There were further fluctuations in form before Border reached new heights to put himself in pole position when a new captain was urgently required. It was often said that he was at his best when faced with adversity, and that was certainly the case when he took over the national team. He had just become captain of Queensland, so he had no great experience of the job. It is fair to say that there were not vast expectations.

It took him time to mould the side, and as he became more comfortable in his role, so the team improved. There was no sudden transformation, and Australia received something of a trouncing in 1985 in England, but he was outstanding with eight first-class centuries on the tour. It was the same story in the series that followed, but the tide was beginning to turn. Border masterminded the World Cup triumph of 1987 and went on to regain the Ashes and retain them twice. Only the West Indies proved immune from the Border effect, and he failed to defeat them in 1992/93 when the opposition got home by one run in Adelaide.

He retired from international cricket in 1994 after yet another successful series in South Africa. At the time, he was the leading run-scorer in Test cricket, he held the record for Test catches, he had played in more Tests, more consecutive Tests and had more Tests as captain than anyone else. No wonder the Australian Player of the Year is now honoured with the Allan Border Medal.

ABOVE
Border with the World Cup, Calcutta 1987.

MIDDLE
Border secures the one-day series against India in 1984.

FAR LEFT
Border finds he can play English bowling with one hand.

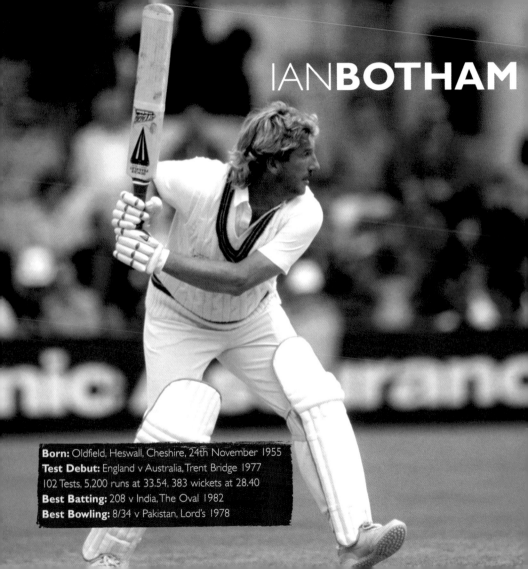

IAN**BOTHAM**

Born: Oldfield, Heswall, Cheshire, 24th November 1955
Test Debut: England v Australia, Trent Bridge 1977
102 Tests, 5,200 runs at 33.54, 383 wickets at 28.40
Best Batting: 208 v India, The Oval 1982
Best Bowling: 8/34 v Pakistan, Lord's 1978

The word "legendary" can be over-used in sport, but surely no England cricketer in living memory deserves the epithet more than Ian Terence Botham. In three Ashes Tests in 1981, immediately after resigning the captaincy of a struggling team in poor personal form, he thrilled an entire nation with his all-round bravado. If his name will forever be associated with his unbeaten 149 at Headingley, he played an innings at Old Trafford that was arguably even greater. In between he charged in like a bull to demolish Australia's batting at Edgbaston, and repeatedly, as throughout his career, took catches that sometimes appeared well out of his reach. Not until England's Ashes triumph in 2005 was cricket again so compelling a spectacle.

BELOW

A triumphant return to Test cricket for England all-rounder Ian Botham, as he dismisses New Zealand's Jeff Crowe to become the highest wicket taker in Test history with 356 victims.

Botham announced himself at international level in 1977 at the age of just 21, with the wicket of Australian great Greg Chappell. If there was an element of good fortune (Chappell dragged the ball on to his stumps) there was nothing fluky about the performances that followed over the next five years. Instinctively and effervescently, Botham became England's match-winner. At Christchurch the following winter he scored a century before taking eight wickets in the match. At Lord's in 1978 he repeated the feat, taking eight for 34 in Pakistan's second innings with his brisk out-swing, the best Test figures of his career. Surely it couldn't get better than this? It did. In Bombay less than two years later, in the Golden Jubilee Test, he scored 114 in between six for 58 and seven for 48. India were nonplussed.

Whether it was right to give Botham the England captaincy on the back of such mesmerising all-round brilliance remains debatable. It was asking a lot of a 24-year-old, against a West Indies side on the threshold of world dominance, and with the home series (which West Indies won 1-0) followed by a return rubber in the Caribbean the following spring. Although Botham continued to pick up

wickets, his batting fell away and he failed to reach 50 after his first Test as captain. Appointed on a match-by-match basis at the start of the 1981 Ashes series, he completed a pair at Lord's after England had gone 1-0 down, resigning before the selectors revealed that they had decided to replace him anyway.

The way was paved for the return of his mentor. Mike Brearley famously offered him the chance to sit out the Headingley Test, laying down a gauntlet which he must have guessed a man of Botham's ebullient character would be sure to take up. Heroic performances followed which turned the rubber on its head, and England ultimately won it 3-1. Botham's 102-ball innings of 118 at Old Trafford prompted the Times to ask whether it was the greatest ever. In his own account of the series, 'Phoenix from the Ashes', Brearley wrote that as the Australians clapped Botham out after his dismissal, "their looks expressed a rare Antipodean awe at the prowess of an Englishman."

Botham would probably have featured in this book had he not set foot on a cricket field again. In the event his Test career lasted more than a decade longer, much to the short-term chagrin of India's bowlers, who were pummelled for three hundreds and five 50s in the home and away series of the following year, including 142 at Kanpur and a Test-best 208 at the Oval. And although he could hardly be blamed for failing to repeat his Ashes exploits Down Under in 1982/3, who else but Botham could have saved the day when Australia were on the verge of stealing

a sensational victory at Melbourne? With help from a butter-fingered Chris Tavare and a cool-headed Geoff Miller, Botham ended a 70-run last wicket partnership between Allan Border and Jeff Thomson to see England home – just – by three runs.

As the years went by the compelling moments became fewer, although as his bowling declined, Botham remained a fearsome striker of the cricket ball for England, Somerset (whom he helped to one-day glory before an acrimonious split in the mid 1980s), Worcestershire and finally Durham. Although he never reached the milestone he must have coveted more than most, a century against the great West Indies, he did manage a dramatic return after a Test ban for allegedly smoking cannabis. He dismissed Bruce Edgar with his first ball, and after two overs he had overtaken Dennis Lillee's world record of 355 Test wickets. "Who writes your scripts?" demanded Graham Gooch. If the cricketing arena is indeed a stage, Botham played his part both on and off it to the outer limits of mortal reach.

FAR LEFT
The classical side-on action of Ian Botham in his pomp.

MIDDLE
Botham in action against Pakistan at Lord's in 1978.

BELOW
Botham relaxes after his 149 not out in the third Ashes Test of 1981.

DON
BRADMAN

Born: Cootamundra, New South Wales, 27th August 1908
Died: Adelaide, South Australia, 25th February 2001
Test Debut: Australia v England, Brisbane 1928
52 Tests, 6,996 runs at 99.94
Best Batting: 334 v England, Headingley 1930

Don Bradman began his Test career at the Exhibition Ground in Brisbane against England in 1928, with scores of 18 and one. He ended it with a much-publicised duck at the Oval in 1948 against the same opposition. In between these two matches, he had the most spectacular career any cricketer – indeed any sportsman – could ever imagine.

BELOW
Don Bradman acknowledges another double-century.

Figures can, and do, sometimes lie, but the statistics associated with Bradman say virtually all there is to say about the greatest batsman of them all. It is generally reckoned that to have enjoyed a substantial Test career, a batsman needs to have averaged 40. To nudge the average past 50 puts him in the top bracket, while to top 60 is extraordinary. Bradman's Test average was 99.94.

It is an oft-told story how he arrived at the Oval for his final Test needing a simple boundary to take him into retirement with an average in excess of 100. With England bowled out for 52 and Australia already having reached 117 when the first wicket fell, it was always likely that it would be his last innings. He was given a standing ovation all the way to the middle, where the England captain, Norman Yardley, called for three cheers. Leg-spinner Eric Hollies was the bowler; Bradman played the first ball but missed the second – a googly – and was bowled.

The shock that engulfed the Oval could be felt around the world, but cricket is a game more capable than most of bringing a humbling mortality even to the greatest player, and Bradman could certainly claim that category for himself. Throughout a first-class career that extended from 1927 to 1949, he averaged a century every three visits to the wicket. His first-class average was 95.14, his top score was 452 not out – a record at the time – while his highest Test innings also established a new benchmark.

With phenomenal statistics like these, it is easy to overlook the quality of the play while marvelling at the magnitude of the

achievement. Bradman's was not necessarily an eye-catching style. He did not blast the ball with great power, and he did not lash it to all parts in the air. In 80 Test innings he hit only six sixes. He played the ball along the ground, relying on timing and placement. It was once said that he had a stroke for every ball, which is why he could score so freely. It was also said that he did not appear to be scoring, although a glance at the board would reveal that he already had 30 to his name when it seemed that he had only just arrived at the wicket.

Bradman was once tested to see if his eyesight was better than anyone else's; it was not. He merely had an outstanding ability to judge the flight of a cricket ball and the most nimble footwork to ensure that he was correctly balanced and positioned to execute his chosen stroke. It is often said that the great players do the simple things better than others. The Bradman formula for success appears simple, but he applied it more diligently than anyone before or since.

Always gifted at sport, he might well have excelled at tennis, golf, athletics or anything else that took his fancy. It was cricket's good fortune to attract his attention. It is the stuff of folklore that he threw a golf ball against a water tank and played the rebound with a cricket stump when a youngster at home in Bowral, some 80 miles from Sydney.

He was 17 when he scored a triple hundred for Bowral and attracted the attention of those higher up the cricketing echelons. He was soon

playing grade cricket in Sydney, making a hundred on his first-class debut for New South Wales, and from there he made his way into the Australian side. After his ordinary start, he was dropped for the second Test but recalled for the third when he scored 79 and 112. He was never dropped again.

He did particularly well against England. At Headingley in 1930, he ended the first day on 309 before going on to the then record score of 334 on the second. In all, he scored 974 runs in that series at an average of 139.14. England became so obsessed with stopping Bradman that the infamous Bodyline strategy was devised to negate him. To a certain degree, it did. In 1932/33 he averaged a mere 56.57!

He had moved from New South Wales to South Australia for the 1935/36 season, taking up the captaincy as soon as he arrived. He was elevated to the same position with the Australian side for the 1936/37 tour by England, and retained the post until he retired. His captaincy reflected his batting in that he won four series and drew one – the 1938 rubber in England. In all, he captained Australia in 24 Tests, losing the first two but only one more, while winning 15.

After retirement, he was equally sagacious as an administrator and selector, while the honours flowed as befitted such a colossus of the game. He was knighted in 1949, and in 1979 was appointed Commander of the Order of Australia. He received a host of additional acclamations as the best Australian sportsman ever, and even as the most influential Australian. It is hard to argue that he was not.

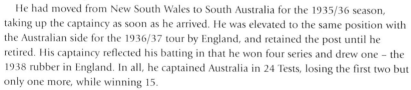

ABOVE
Bradman with a much-loved bat in 1930.

LEFT
More runs for The Don.

FAR LEFT
Bradman returns to the pavilion past admiring fans.

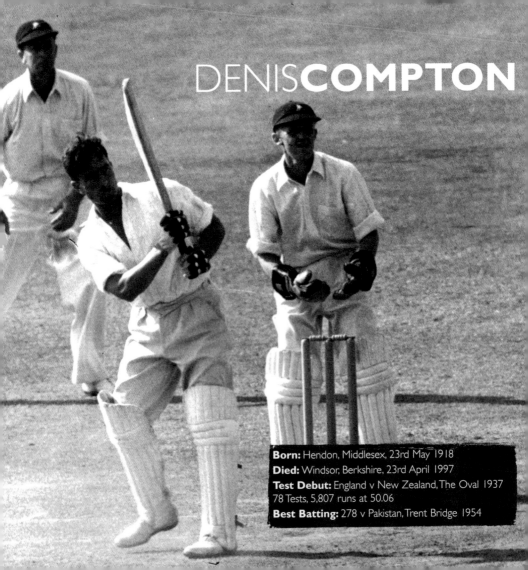

DENIS**COMPTON**

Born: Hendon, Middlesex, 23rd May 1918
Died: Windsor, Berkshire, 23rd April 1997
Test Debut: England v New Zealand, The Oval 1937
78 Tests, 5,807 runs at 50.06
Best Batting: 278 v Pakistan, Trent Bridge 1954

One of the finest of many vintage (and some no doubt apocryphal) stories about Denis Compton was told by the legendary cricket commentator Brian Johnston. It concerned a party at Lord's for Compton's 50th birthday. As the champagne corks popped in the Middlesex office, the telephone rang. "It's for you, Denis," he was told. He went to take the call, and returned looking a bit glum. "Who was it?" he was asked. "It was my mother. She says I'm only 49."

True or not, it characterises the endearing vagueness of the cricketer who did more than anyone to revive English spirits after the Second World War. If it was feasible to be more than the complete batsman, Denis Charles Scott Compton managed it by sheer audacity. His sweep, often played brazenly late, was his trademark, although he possessed a sublime cover drive and was an accomplished stroke player all around the wicket. Like Viv Richards a generation later, he was sure footed enough to keep the bowler guessing, moving around his crease in all manner of directions. The result was untutored artistry on an exalted level that had to be seen to be believed.

Cricket was in Compton's blood; his father and brother were both keen participants, and Denis was in his father's team by the age of 12. At 18 he got his first game for Middlesex, and although he started at number 11, by the end of the 1936 season he had passed a thousand runs. And he couldn't just bat; he was a naturally athletic

fielder when concentrating (he took 425 first-class catches), and his unorthodox left-arm spin was to reap 622 first-class wickets, 25 of them in Tests. He was also a fine footballer, playing in a cup final for Arsenal, and wartime internationals for England. But for the war, he might well have won a full cap.

Although he made his Test debut in 1937 – with 65 against New Zealand – Compton's great years came in the wake of the war. In 1947 he scored 3,816 runs, including 18 centuries, two of them in the same Test against Australia at the start of

the year. Back home he decimated South Africa with 65, 163, 208, 115, 6, 30, 53 and 113. But even such sensational statistics cannot convey the show-man-like flair with which the runs were scored, enrapturing the cricket-starved crowds who flocked to watch. Two more big hundreds followed in the 1948 Ashes series, and the following winter he took just three hours to score 300 at Benoni in South Africa.

Shortly afterwards an old football injury to his knee resurfaced, reducing Compton's mobility. It did not prevent a prolific series against New Zealand in 1950, but he failed to reach 50 on the ensuing Ashes tour. However he savoured the most magical of moments in 1953 when, with his "Middlesex Twin" Bill Edrich at the other end, he hit the winning runs to ensure England's Ashes triumph. Runs flowed in the Caribbean that winter and in 1954 he amassed his best Test score of 278 against Pakistan. Compton himself regarded the 53 he made on a damp wicket at the Oval later in that series as one of his best innings.

By his standards he was again below par in Australia, but South Africa suffered sorely at his hands again in 1955. In November of that year his right kneecap was surgically removed (it now resides in the Lord's museum) but he was able to play his final Test against the Old Enemy the following summer, scoring 94 and 35 not out. After the winter tour of South Africa, Compton bowed out of Test cricket.

By then he had an agent, Bagenal Harvey, who not only did the deal that identified his client as the "Brylcreem Boy" but also brought a semblance of organisation to Compton's life. Poor timekeeping had always been a consequence of his vagueness; heaven knows how he would have managed current rules on punctuality. Another trait was his erratic calling and running between the wickets. As Trevor Bailey once asserted: "A call from Denis was merely the basis for negotiation." He even contrived to run his brother Leslie out in his benefit match.

Compton lived life to the full after retirement. He was awarded a CBE, wrote and broadcast about cricket, and turned out for the Lord's Taverners. When he died, paradoxically as spring was ushering in a new cricket season, there were more applications to attend his memorial service at Westminster Abbey than for any in 30 years. If Len Hutton was the peerless batsman of his age, no one played more enchantingly, or was more widely loved, than Denis Compton.

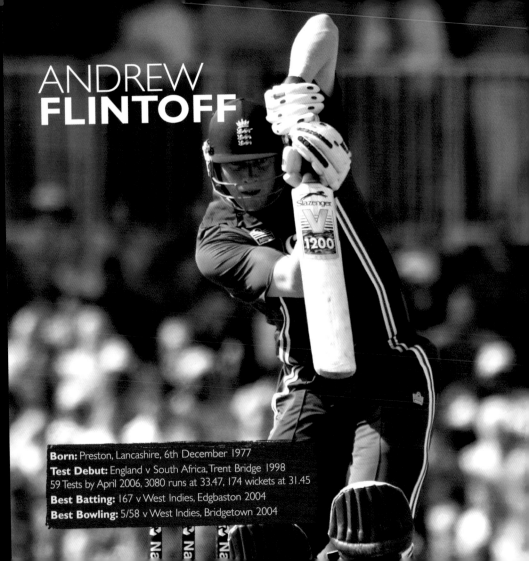

ANDREW
FLINTOFF

Born: Preston, Lancashire, 6th December 1977

Test Debut: England v South Africa, Trent Bridge 1998
59 Tests by April 2006, 3080 runs at 33.47, 174 wickets at 31.45

Best Batting: 167 v West Indies, Edgbaston 2004

Best Bowling: 5/58 v West Indies, Bridgetown 2004

There was a strict criterion for inclusion in this book as a cricket legend. Players had to have already achieved greatness. In the case of Andrew Flintoff, we have a legend in the making. He does not yet hold records or, apart from in the physical sense, tower head and shoulders above others in the game, but there is an aura about him that transcends the normal to elevate him into a special category of cricketer.

He went through a lot early in his career, which perhaps shaped the character that appears on the field today, for not all of it made for an easy ride to the top. There are some players who impress at an early age merely because of physical maturity in advance of their years. The young Flintoff impressed not only for his size but also for his precocious talent. A fast bowler and big-hitting batsman, he had to shelve his bowling aspirations while his body became strong enough to cope with the enormous strains that were placed upon it.

He emerged through the Lancashire youth teams and attracted the attention of age group selectors. However, by the time he was captaining the England Under-19s, it appeared that he might gain top honours as a batsman alone because of back injuries that threatened his future as a bowler.

The path to the top was not smooth. After his Under-19 appearances, he progressed to the England A team for a tour to Kenya and Sri Lanka in early 1998. He did well enough to be propelled into the Test side that summer, at a time when youngsters were not necessarily made welcome in the England dressing room. He showed promise against South Africa in his first Test but in the second, recorded a pair and took no wickets in either innings. England won both matches but Flintoff was dropped.

Back in the ranks with England A, he toured Zimbabwe and South Africa where, after some initial problems, he came of age.

He sowed doubts on that tour by getting himself out when set, the result of poor shot selection. Twice in a match against a ZCU President's XI in Kwekwe he holed out at long on and long off. It appeared that he might never learn the lessons that were so obvious. However, later in the tour in Johannesburg, he played a dominant innings against a Gauteng XI that showed his full potential.

He went to South Africa again the following winter with the full England side, and to Sharjah to make his one-day international debut, but struggled to find his best form. He was overweight and apparently lacking in motivation as a persistent back injury restricted his bowling and mobility. Back home, he played a one-day international against Zimbabwe at Old Trafford where he did not bowl, but was named man of the match for an innings of 42 not out. He accepted the award with the words: "Not bad for a fat lad." Flintoff appeared about to be consigned to the scrap heap of unfulfilled potential that has littered English cricket over the years when he took himself in hand, spent time with the Academy and emerged the stronger for it.

He was called up for the tour of India and New Zealand in the winter of 2001/02 and, after a torrid time against the Indian spinners, made an impact in the one-day internationals and showed increasing maturity in New Zealand with his maiden Test hundred. He established himself in the Test team in 2003 with an outstanding series against South Africa, scoring 423 runs at 52.87, although his bowling average was even higher. He was labelled as an unlucky bowler, but at least he was bowling again.

Having missed out on the 2002/03 Ashes series due to a hernia operation from which he failed to recover, despite travelling to

The Little Book of **CRICKET** LEGENDS

Australia, he was keen to show his mettle in what he regarded as the true cricketing test. He did not disappoint in England's triumph of 2005. For many, it was Flintoff's triumph. 24 wickets in the series at 27.29 and 402 runs at 40.20 propelled him to national and international stardom.

It was his ebullient character that shone through during the Ashes series and made him so admired. The England and Wales Cricket Board wanted heroes with whom the young could identify and here they had a ready-made candidate. His cheery personality, folksy wit and imposing physical presence meant that Freddie's was the name on everyone's lips. Even when he "over-celebrated" after the final Oval Test, his behaviour was restrained enough to attract sympathy for his hangover rather than criticism for getting it in the first place.

He was selected for the Rest of the World team to play Australia in both Test and one-day internationals, like the rest of the Ashes-winners he was dubbed an MBE, and won just about every sports personality of the year award going, not to mention the Wisden award for Leading Cricketer of the World in 2005. He deserved it, because here was a character who would always rely on his cricketing ability to maintain his celebrity status.

This he showed in abundance when he toured India at the start of 2006. Already the key player in the England team as major batsman, strike bowler, stock bowler and reliable slip fielder, he took on the additional burden of the captaincy when the need arose. He was a natural leader, showing that while he can be relied upon to serve his country in every capacity for the foreseeable future, he will remain Big Freddie from Lancashire however great the pressures of fame become.

ABOVE
Flintoff in one-day international action against Bangladesh at Trent Bridge in 2005.

MIDDLE
Four runs out of 102 during Flintoff's brilliant innings against Australia at Trent Bridge in 2005.

FAR LEFT
Flintoff in action for the Rest of the World XI in Australia in 2005.

SUNIL
GAVASKAR

Born: Bombay, Maharashtra, 10th July 1949
Test Debut: West Indies v India, Port of Spain 1971
125 Tests 10,122 Test runs at 51.12
Best Batting: 236* v West Indies, Madras 1983

It would be very easy to explain Sunil Manohar Gavaskar's inclusion in a list of legends merely by listing statistical achievements that are virtually unparalleled in modern cricket. They are all there and must be mentioned, but to confine an appreciation of the man to mere figures would fail to portray the true measure of his greatness.

BELOW
Sunil Gavaskar
sweeps towards his
century against
Australia in 1979.

In Indian society, Gavaskar is often referred to as a demi-god. It is even debatable whether the prefix "demi" is necessary. Suffice to say that this friendly, cheerful, likeable man deserves all the plaudits that come his way. To retain all those adjectives under the intense public scrutiny and intrusive interest that he endures in his native India is a remarkable achievement.

It is a revelation to see how he is treated in his homeland. Try travelling to an airport with him in the same car. Get out and collect your luggage from the boot before making your way to the fast-track boarding channel. Whisked through, you are first on the plane – you think. But no; when you board you will find Gavaskar already in his seat, as if he de-materialise in the car and re-materialised on the aircraft. It is an extraordinary performance.

Gavaskar's status arises from his genius as a batsman. He might be short in stature at under five feet, five inches, but he was a batting giant. His nimble footwork enabled him to manufacture the length of the ball. He seldom hooked, but played more or less every other stroke in the book with technical perfection that was a wonder to behold. Not the first, nor the last to be labelled the "Little Master", he was indeed a master of batting.

He had appeared in only six first-class matches, with three centuries to his credit, when he was selected for the Indian tour to the West Indies in 1970/71. He was 17 at the time. He missed the first Test in Jamaica through injury, but marked his debut with 65 and 67 not out in the

second Test, India's first-ever win against the West Indies. He did not look back. In the remainder of the series he scored 116, 64 not out, 1,117 not out, 124 and 220. 774 runs, dismissed only three times and boasting a Test average of 154.80.

So he continued, using his immense powers of concentration and technique clinically to dismantle all the great bowling attacks arrayed against him. He practiced diligently. He was not renowned as a fast run-scorer, particularly after batting through 60 overs for 36 not out in the first World Cup match at Lord's in 1975, when he thought England's total of 334 was too great to chase. However, he would end any net session by practicing straight sixes, to the delight of the locals on his home grounds.

His ability to score quickly manifested itself at the Oval in 1979. India were set 483 to beat England in 498 minutes; Gavaskar responded with an innings of 221 that took India to within nine runs of an unlikely victory. The match was drawn, but Gavaskar had played a majestic innings of immense charm and character.

At various stages of his career he held the record for the most Test runs and the most Test centuries. When he

equalled Sir Donald Bradman's record of 29 Test centuries, he was the first to point out that he had taken 95 matches to do so while Bradman set the mark in only 52. Gavaskar still holds the record for the number of separate hundreds in Tests, while it was once suggested that he held the record for breaking batting records. That puts his career in perspective.

Apart from the World Cup debacle in 1975 at Lord's, the only other time he acted below the highest standard of dignity was at Melbourne in 1981. On one of several occasions he was called upon to lead his country, he was emerging from a bad spell when he was given out lbw to Dennis Lillee.

Such was his disgust that he ordered his batting partner to leave the field with him. Had he done so, India would not have levelled the series.

That was not typical Gavaskar. He made friends and runs wherever he went, including one season for Somerset in the County Championship and in all the Test countries around the world. Furthermore, he achieved his records while opening the batting against some of the great fast bowlers of the age. Few easy runs were to be had, but then Gavaskar did not need easy runs. When talent and application come together in one such neat package, there was an inevitability about the result.

ADAM
GILCHRIST

Born: Bellingen, New South Wales, 14th November 1971

Test Debut: Australia v Pakistan, Brisbane 1999
79 Tests by the end of 2005, 4,918 runs at 50.18, 333 dismissals

Best Batting: 204* v South Africa, Johannesburg 2002

A modern-day England wicket-keeper said of Adam Gilchrist: "He's put the cat among the pigeons, and put us 'keepers under a lot of pressure." When Gilchrist preys on an attack, fielders need the agility of cats to contain him. Nothing could better illustrate the colossal impact made by the New South Welshman on cricket in general and the role of the wicket-keeper/batsman in particular, which he has taken to an unprecedented level simply by the pace at which he scores his copious runs. Kept out of the Australian Test team until he was nearly 28 by the consistency of his record-breaking predecessor Ian Healy, Adam Craig Gilchrist has since played as if there is no time to be lost.

"Just hit the ball" is the batting gospel from which he has been unswerving since making his debut (as a specialist) for his home state in 1992/93. Determined to win a regular place as a wicket-keeper/batsman, he moved to Western Australia after just two seasons, quickly displacing the former international Tim Zoehrer. His one-day international debut followed in 1996 and less than a year later the position, amid some controversy, had become his own. Upon Healy's retirement in 1999 Gilchrist gave immediate notice of his unique batting credentials, scoring 81 from just 88 balls on Test debut at the 'Gabba against Pakistan.

To confirm the explosion of a meteor upon the Test firmament, Gilchrist shattered a Pakistan attack including Wasim Akram, Waqar Younis and Shoaib Akhtar with an unbeaten 149 in the next game at Hobart, again at almost a run a ball. Facing defeat when he walked out to bat, Australia instead snatched a sensational win that also secured them the series. As Steve Waugh's men marched towards the status of immortals, primarily through their ability to win consistently by the pace at which they scored their runs, Gilchrist was already the team's heartbeat.

As a wicket-keeper, he may not quite possess the acrobatic agility of Alan Knott,

BELOW
Adam Gilchrist – a
fixture behind the
stumps for Australia.

Healy or another great Australian, Rod Marsh, but Gilchrist is nonetheless infectiously enthusiastic, robustly athletic and almost entirely reliable. He is forthright in his encouragement of individual bowlers, and offers welcome advice to his skipper from a viewpoint that is invariably valuable. Australia's vice-captain for much of his career, he has stepped up on several occasions, most famously when Australia won in India in 2004 for the first time in 35 years, avenging their defeat in the classic encounter of 2001.

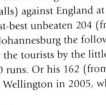

But it is his batting that transfigures Gilchrist from a mere great to a living legend. He possesses that priceless ability to change a match in a session. Scrupulously fair (he once walked when given not out in a World Cup semi-final), he appears merciless when he is annihilating an attack. Witness his 152 (from 143 balls) against England at Edgbaston in 2001, or his Test-best unbeaten 204 (from 213) against South Africa in Johannesburg the following year, which set up victory for the tourists by the little matter of an innings and 360 runs. Or his 162 (from 146) against New Zealand at Wellington in 2005, which

paved the way for another victory. What a performer to have coming in at number seven!

He can be vulnerable to deliveries bowled from round the wicket and angling away from him, an Achilles' heel primarily exposed by Andrew Flintoff (and some brilliant close catching) in the great Ashes contest of 2005. Gilchrist failed to reach a half-century in the series, an almost unimaginable rarity. This dip in form was by no means the least significant factor in Australia's surrender of the famous little urn that they had held, metaphorically at least, for 16 years. But he was back into his stride later in the year, falling just six short of a century in the one-off Test against an ICC World XI, and with 86 against South Africa at the SCG.

FAR LEFT
Another one-day hundred for Gilchrist, this time against Sri Lanka at Sydney in 1999.

MIDDLE
Gilchrist at his best at Brisbane in 1999.

BELOW
Australia top the cricketing world – it's official. Gilchrist shows off the trophy in 2002.

Gilchrist's influence on one-day internationals has been no less seismic. Initially going in at number seven, he was soon promoted to open, enabling him to exercise his unique brand of aggression with the fielding restrictions in place. He scores at a rate of around 94 per hundred balls, a statistic enough on its own to assure him of a place in the putative best ever one-day World XI. No one in the modern era, with the possible exception of Viv Richards, can have instilled such trepidation in the heart of a bowler – or such expectations beyond the boundary – as Adam Gilchrist on his way to the crease. No wonder his teammate Justin Langer described him as a freak.

GRAHAM
GOOCH

Born: Whipps Cross, Leytonstone, Essex, 23rd July 1953
Test Debut: England v Australia, Edgbaston 1975
118 Tests, 8,900 runs at 42.58
Best Batting: 333 v India, Lord's 1990

You can just imagine the type of aura that will surround Graham Gooch in the years to come. "That Goochie; he used to say when he was going out to get a hundred – and did!" Perhaps that is going a little too far, because he did not forecast each of the 128 first-class hundreds that he compiled over a long career that saw him score more runs in top-class cricket than anyone else in the history of the game.

BELOW
Graham Gooch during his first Test century against Australia at the Oval in 1985. He made 196.

He thought he had scored his hundredth hundred on a South African Breweries 'rebel' tour in 1982. Despite the fact that the opposition contained bowlers of the quality of Mike Procter, Garth le Roux, Clive Rice and Vincent van der Bijl, the International Cricket Council had deemed that the match was not to be accorded first-class status. Gooch shrugged off the disappointment and is reported to have said in that rather high-pitched voice that belied his physical presence: "I'll just have to go out and get 100 against Cambridge University at Fenner's when I get home." It goes without saying that he did just that.

Graham Alan Gooch was marked out as something rather special as soon as he made his way into the Essex side and, at just 21, he was propelled into the Test team. In retrospect it was possibly a little too soon, but England wanted new, young blood to take the attack to the Australians in 1975 and that was exactly the way Gooch batted.

He used a massive bat that he wielded with a purpose, but the likes of Dennis Lillee, Jeff Thompson and Max Walker were a little too much for him and he got a pair on debut at Edgbaston. He did slightly better at Lord's, with 6 and 31, but that was to be the end of his England involvement until 1978, when he had re-invented himself as an opening rather than middle-order batsman, and marked his return to the Test side with an innings of 54 against Pakistan. He established himself in the team, took 91 not out off a decent

GRAHAM**GOOCH**

New Zealand attack and reached 99 against Australia in Melbourne in 1980 before being run out. It was not until his 36th Test innings that he finally recorded a hundred, against the all-conquering West Indians.

By now he had tightened his technique with obvious benefits, but at the time when he should have been at his peak as a Test batsman, not to say a murderous one-day player, he went on the rebel tour to South Africa. He was lost to international cricket until the series against Australia in 1985. The highlight of his return came in the sixth Test at the Oval, where he savaged the Australian attack. He scored 196 while putting on 351 with David Gower for the second wicket.

His first foray into international captaincy was in somewhat bizarre circumstances. He was successful as Essex captain, guiding them to the County Championship in his first year in charge when he was at the top of his game. When Mike Gatting lost the captaincy following his spat with Shakoor Rana and an alleged dalliance with a barmaid, both John Emburey and Chris Cowdrey were tried, before the selectors eventually turned to Gooch as a stopgap.

Gower resumed the captaincy when the Australians next visited, in 1989, and Gooch was suffering a dip in form. His somewhat idiosyncratic upright stance had started to let him down as he fell across his stumps to be lbw on numerous occasions, to Terry Alderman in particular. But Gooch was back in charge for the tour to the Caribbean the next winter, and stayed in post for another 32 Tests.

The Little Book of **CRICKET** LEGENDS

In 1990 at Lord's, he played a gargantuan innings against India. At a time when the highest individual innings in Test cricket was Sobers' 365 against Pakistan, Gooch reached 333 on only the second afternoon before fatigue got the better of him and he was bowled. Not as great in terms of runs, his 154 against the West Indies at Headingley the following summer was a match-winning effort that might well rate as his finest performance in Test cricket.

With limited resources, his tenure was not marked by spectacular success in terms of results, winning ten and drawing 12, but he instilled a strict fitness regime in the England team to set the standards in years to come. He had always maintained strong links with his beloved Essex even when immersed in England matters, and in one season scored at least one fifty in every match he played for the county between international commitments.

He continued with Essex after retiring from international cricket in 1995, before admitting that "the tank was empty" at the age of 44. After all those runs, even a fitness fanatic who ran marathons was entitled to put his feet up. He performed some coaching duties, served time as a selector and now, as well as playing a role with Essex, surprises people who knew him merely as a rather dour and straight-faced individual. He is a media pundit and makes humourous appearances on the after-dinner circuit, remembering his scores on his Test debut in a splendidly self-deprecating way. "They stare back at me every time I sign my surname."

FAR LEFT
The end of the innings. Gooch returns to the pavilion for the last time in a Test, at Perth in 1995.

MIDDLE
Gooch on his way to 333 against India at Lord's in 1990.

BELOW
Gooch the coach in 1999.

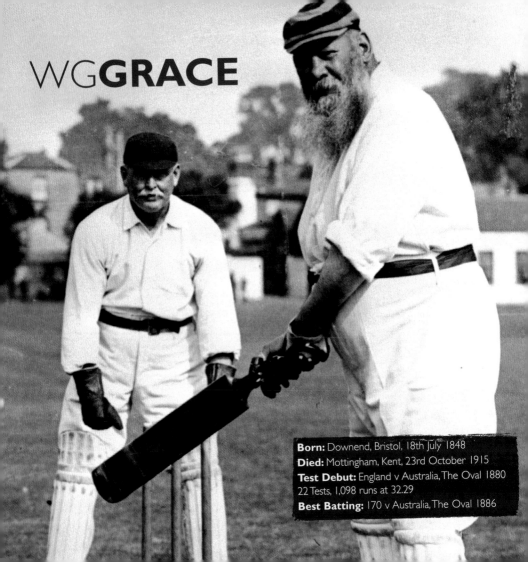

WG**GRACE**

Born: Downend, Bristol, 18th July 1848
Died: Mottingham, Kent, 23rd October 1915
Test Debut: England v Australia, The Oval 1880
22 Tests, 1,098 runs at 32.29
Best Batting: 170 v Australia, The Oval 1886

Difficult though it is reliably to portray a legend barely seen in action by anyone alive, W.G.'s statistical record, combined with his immortal status as cricket's special ancestor, makes an irrefutable case for inclusion. From the moment when, at the age of just 18, he scored an unbeaten 224 for England against Surrey at the Oval (in a match he left briefly to win a quarter-mile hurdles championship at Crystal Palace), he was the dominant figure in English cricket for four decades. In an age of uncovered and capricious pitches, the "Champion" scored over 54,000 first-class runs at an average a shade under 40. His round-arm bowling accounted for more than 2,800 wickets and he held over 870 catches. His burly figure was probably the most familiar of his day, and his bushy beard remains the most recognisable in cricket's history.

The fourth of five brothers, William Gilbert Grace was coached from an early age in the garden of the family home near Bristol, and was already making a formidable impression as a teenager. At just 17 he took 13 wickets for the Gentlemen v Players of the South; over 41 years he was to make over 6,000 runs for the Gentlemen, including 15 hundreds. His two greatest seasons came in 1871 and 1876. In the first, he reached the astounding total of 2,739 runs, with ten centuries and an average of 78. Although he fell marginally short of that aggregate in 1876, he hit the purplest of patches between the 11th and 18th August.

Three prolific innings mark that period, the first triple century in first-class cricket – 344 for MCC against Kent – followed by 177 for Gloucestershire against Nottinghamshire at Clifton. His subsequent unbeaten 318 against Yorkshire on a Cheltenham belter stood as a county record for 128 years, until the New Zealander Craig Spearman broke it in 2004. As he went in, in the high-pitched, squeaky voice that so contrasted with his physical presence, Grace warned: "You'll have to get me out today. I shan't get myself out." By stumps Yorkshire's attack was in tatters. In just eight days W.G. had amassed 839 runs at the none-too-shabby average of 419.5. To round things off neatly in September, he made 400 not out in an exhibition match against a Grimsby XXII, all fielding, to celebrate the birth of his son.

Although Grace's Test career spanned 20 seasons, he made only one Test tour of Australia and appeared in just 22 games in all, 13 of them as captain. He began imposingly, with 152 in his maiden Test innings at the Oval in 1880 (the first Test

hundred for England). Two of W.G.'s brothers also played in that match, E.M., whose nickname of "The Coroner" derived from his profession – he once had a corpse put on ice until he could attend to it after close of play – and G.F., Fred, who tragically died of pneumonia two weeks later. W.G. himself outshone his maiden innings six years later with 170, also at the Oval. He reached the age of 51 before retiring from Tests in 1899, saying: "The ground was getting too far away."

Genius though he was, Grace undoubtedly stretched the rules of the game. Clean bowled early in a minor match, he replaced the bails and batted on, saying that the crowd had come to watch him and not the bowler. When given out on another occasion he remonstrated: "Shan't have it, can't have it, won't have it!" "But you'll have to have it!" was the riposte, and back to the pavilion he had to go. For an amateur he was also unashamedly mercenary, charging a fee of £1,500 from the organisers of his first tour of Australia in 1873/4, and regularly collecting testimonials.

Perhaps Grace's most astonishing season came in 1895, when the "Old Man" – he was 47 – managed 2,346 runs, including his hundredth hundred when he made 288 against Somerset. After playing his final first-class match for the Gentlemen of England in 1908, Grace died a year after the outbreak of the Great War. His reputation is measured by this extract of the

LEFT

The sight opponents dreaded. The Doctor sets out to examine another attack.

FAR LEFT

W.G. Grace – the thinking bowler.

obituary written for The Times by Sir Arthur Conan Doyle. "To those who knew him he was more than a great cricketer. He had many of the characteristics of a great man. There was a masterful personality and a large direct simplicity and frankness which, combined with his huge frame, swarthy features, bushy beard and somewhat lumbering carriage, made an impression which could never be forgotten."

RICHARD**HADLEE**

Born: Christchurch, New Zealand, 3rd July 1951
Test Debut: New Zealand v Pakistan, Wellington 1973
86 Tests, 431 wickets at 22.29
Best Bowling: 9/52 v Australia, Brisbane 1985

Richard John Hadlee had cricketing pedigree. His father, Walter, had his career interrupted by the Second World War, but became captain of a weak Test side in the 1940s. He had two brothers, Dayle and Barry, who both represented New Zealand on the cricket field, and even his ex-wife, Karen, represented New Zealand Women on one occasion. Richard, however, was not only head and shoulders above his family members, but also above most cricketers of his type.

Quick bowlers, it is said, hunt best in pairs, but Hadlee was virtually a lone ranger throughout his long and distinguished career. Not especially quick in his pomp, but with quite immaculate control and all the arts and crafts in the trade, he became one of the most consistent and successful fast-medium bowlers that cricket has seen.

His abilities as a batsman should not be underestimated either, although he was considered vulnerable against raw pace. Who is not? Below international cricket he could be considered an all-rounder. In Test cricket he averaged 27.16 with two hundreds and 15 fifties. In all first-class cricket his average rose to 31.71 with 14 hundreds and 59 fifties. His highest score was 210 not out, for Nottinghamshire against Middlesex at Lord's in 1984, when the Middlesex attack consisted of Wayne Daniel, Norman Cowans, Neil Williams, John Emburey and Phil Edmonds.

1984 was one of Hadlee's most influential years for his adopted county. By then he had helped them to their first Championship title for 52 years in 1981, an achievement to be repeated in 1987. In 1984, in 24 Championship matches, he took 117 wickets and scored 1,179 runs, becoming the first player to complete the double in an English season since 1967. Hadlee was revered by the people of Nottinghamshire, hardly surprising when you consider that his worst bowling average in ten seasons at Trent Bridge was 17.

He made his debut for his home province of Canterbury, where his two

brothers were already playing, in 1971/72. With a long run and long hair, he was the epitome of the wild fast bowler. He was wild, too, sacrificing the accuracy that was to become his trademark for pace, not necessarily with outstanding results.

He played three first-class matches in his debut season, and in 1972/73 he appeared in six matches but trebled his wicket-taking to finish with 30 at 18.33. He also made his Test debut against Pakistan and was selected for the tour of England that followed.

Again, he played in just the first Test of the series, but by the time New Zealand visited Australia in 1973/74 Hadlee was established as his country's leading new-ball bowler. His figures did not always reflect the fact, but when he got it right, he was a real handful. It was a deeply analytical mind, so focused on his bowling, that led to dramatic improvements in his game.

Hadlee always had a classical, side-on high action, but it was not yet the reliable, repeating model that was to give such consistency and allow him to achieve such accuracy and command of the ball. He realised that if he continued to run a long way and bowl at top pace the whole time, his career would not be long enough to reach the goals he set himself. The answer? Cut down his run, reduce pace and master control.

The results were spectacular. On any surface giving a modicum of help he could be unplayable. Few batsmen could get on top of him, while the pressure

his accuracy created was always likely to produce wickets. It was quite a feat to change his mindset in this way. Patience did not come naturally to the young tearaway, and to develop an approach that relied on his powers of concentration outlasting those of the batsmen required great application.

His attributes were revealed to their full potential in Brisbane in 1985. Hadlee took nine for 52 in the first innings; the irony was that Vaughan Brown's only Test wicket robbed him of all ten. After scoring 54, he took six for 71 in the second innings. He might not have been able to reproduce such figures at will, but he took five or more wickets in an innings on no less than 36 occasions in Test cricket.

Milestones came and went. Hadlee became the leading Test wicket-taker in 1988, went past the then magical 400 mark in 79 matches, and by the time he retired in 1990, already knighted, he had amassed 431. He did not play first-class cricket after bowing out of the Test arena, but he still turned out for his old school's veterans side in presidents grade cricket in Christchurch, appearing on public park pitches. Casual passers-by must have blinked to see a legend in action; batsmen could never afford to do likewise.

WALTER
HAMMOND

Born: Buckland, Dover, Kent, 19th June 1903
Died: Kloof, Natal, South Africa, 1st July 1965
Test Debut: South Africa v England, Johannesburg 1927
85 Tests, 7,249 runs at 58.45, 83 wickets at 37.8
Best Batting: 336* v New Zealand, Auckland 1933

It is a remarkable coincidence that two of the greatest cricketers in the game's history played for Gloucestershire. For W.G. Grace this was entirely logical, given his birth in Bristol. Walter Reginald Hammond, however, was born in Kent and taken to Hong Kong and then Malta in childhood before his parents returned to England, but not to Kent, when he was 11. He was sent to board at Cirencester Grammar School, whence he gravitated to Gloucestershire. For cricket lovers in and around the county, it must have been the most felicitous accident imaginable.

Kent's vain efforts to secure Hammond's return there resulted in him being forced, at the age of 18, to serve a two-year qualification. It was an unfortunate delay in the development of a player who, to paraphrase Shakespeare, was to bestride the cricket world like a colossus. Tall and strong, he batted with poise and grace, particularly against spin, while in the slips he made even the most difficult catches seem almost effortless. A resourceful bowler, particularly with the new ball, he might have been one of the game's greatest all-rounders but for a customary reluctance to turn his arm over.

Hammond's first tour was with the MCC to the West Indies in 1925/26, where he scored an unbeaten 238 in the first of three unofficial "Tests". He also contracted a near-fatal disease from which he took months to recover. But in 1927 he emphasised that recovery was complete with 1,000 runs in May, and took such toll of a strong Lancashire attack at Old Trafford that he reached 187 in just three hours. His Test debut came the same year in South Africa and included a half century as well as, ironically, his best Test bowling figures of five for 36.

Such success paled by comparison, however, with Hammond's first tour of Australia the following winter. 251 in the second Test at Sydney, 200 in the third at Melbourne and in the fourth, at Adelaide, he followed an unbeaten 119 with 177. He made 905 runs in the rubber, still an England record. On his next tour Down Under in 1932/33, he followed two hundreds in the Bodyline series with 227 and 336 not out in New Zealand, breaking Don Bradman's record individual Test score of 334, made at Headingley less than three years earlier.

Curiously, such riches amassed overseas were rarely achieved in Tests at home, although Hammond hit a purple patch against India in 1936, with 167 and 217 in successive Tests. His innings of 240 against Australia at Lord's in 1938 was more memorable still. With England reduced to 31 for three by the young fast bowler Ernie

McCormick, Hammond's response – he was now England's captain – was contained in a ferocious volley of his trademark offside strokes. He hit 32 boundaries in a chanceless display that brought him a standing ovation when he was dismissed six hours later. There was another prolific tour of South Africa before the intervention of war.

It says much for Hammond's pedigree that he was able to resume cricket afterwards. He led England in the victory "Tests" against Australia in 1945 and the next year, at the age of 43, scored 1,783 first-class runs (topping the averages at 84.9). But the heady days could not be relived at international level. Just two half centuries came in his remaining eight Tests, one in his final innings in New Zealand at the end of the ill-starred tour of 1946/47. By this time Hammond was suffering from fibrositis and had problems in his personal life. England were roundly beaten in Australia and on his return home, he announced his retirement.

His life after cricket was not easy. After moving with his second wife,

Sybil, to her native South Africa, he embarked on two unsuccessful business ventures and was seriously injured in a road accident. His death from a heart attack in 1965 left his family in financial disarray, and with distressing bathos, his cricketing trophies were returned to England to be sold at auction. The buyers, as David Foot wrote in the Guardian, "paid, in an inexplicable way, to purge their guilt – as cricket lovers – at the thought that the auction should have been held at all."

In first-class cricket, Hammond scored 50,493 runs with 167 centuries, took 732 wickets and held 819 catches. But as Sir Neville Cardus wrote, statistics only tell so much. "You might as well count the notes of Beethoven, or measure the Elgin Marbles." R.C. Robertson-Glasgow summed up the man who habitually sported a blue handkerchief while batting thus: "He enriched the game with a grace, simplicity and nobility that may never be seen again."

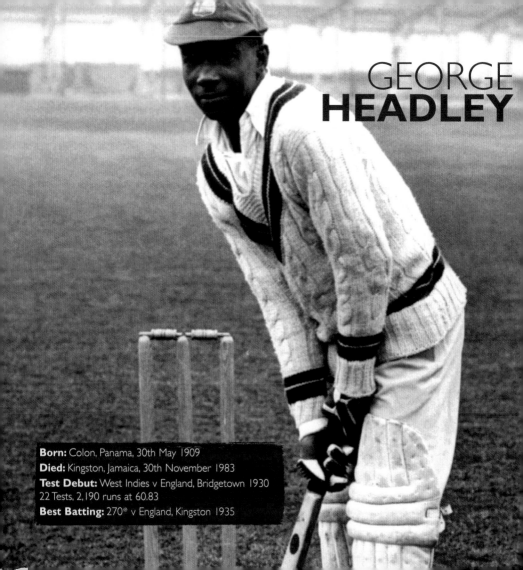

GEORGE
HEADLEY

Born: Colon, Panama, 30th May 1909
Died: Kingston, Jamaica, 30th November 1983
Test Debut: West Indies v England, Bridgetown 1930
22 Tests, 2,190 runs at 60.83
Best Batting: 270* v England, Kingston 1935

There was a time when some respected judges described George Headley as the "Black Bradman". Supporters in the Caribbean countered by describing the great Sir Donald as the "White Headley". From a totally different and more colourful background than his Australian counterpart, Headley nonetheless came as close as anyone to matching Bradman's remarkable statistical feats.

Headley did not have as many opportunities as Bradman to play at the highest level, for the West Indies at the time were granted fewer matches by the established Test powers. His span of 24 years from first Test to last allowed him only 22 games, while Bradman played 52 in his 20-year career. For ten years before the Second World War, Headley never missed a Test for the West Indies. After the war, he played in only two further Tests because of a chronic back condition. At the start of his career, it was the vagaries of West Indian cricket politics that kept him out of the side.

It was purely by chance that George Alphonso Headley began an unparalleled dynasty of Test cricketers. His son, Ronald George Alphonso, appeared twice for the West Indies. He played most of his cricket in England for Worcestershire, and was called into the touring team of 1973. Grandson Dean Warren Headley played 15 Tests for England between 1997 and 1999 before he was forced into early retirement by a persistent back injury – just like grandad all those years earlier.

It is not often that the United States features prominently in cricket history, but the Headley story owes everything to the fact that the US immigration department were tardy in issuing a visa to allow George entry to study dentistry. Born in Panama, he went to his mother's native island of Jamaica when he was ten and soon showed a rare talent for the game. At 18 he was due to take up his studies, but the lack of a visa meant that he stayed to appear for Jamaica in two matches, against a team of touring English cricketers under the captaincy of the Hon. Lionel Tennyson.

Headley announced himself with an innings of 211 which was described by Wisden as "containing many strokes and with only one chance." To show it was no fluke, he followed it up with 71. Dentistry and the USA would have to wait, even though for some unfathomable reason he was not selected for the first West Indian Test team that toured England in 1928.

The West Indies lost all three of the matches in that series by an innings. What made the difference a year or so later when England became the West Indies' first Test opponents in the Caribbean? Headley. On his debut he scored 21 in the first innings and

176 in the second. He failed in the second Test in Port of Spain which the West Indies lost, but played a significant role in Georgetown in the next match with innings of 114 and 112 as the West Indies recorded their first Test victory. He was no less influential in securing the draw in the fourth Test in Kingston, where he scored 223 in the second innings. Headley finished his first Test series with an average of 87.88.

He found life a little more difficult on the tour of Australia that followed, but he still reached centuries in Brisbane and Sydney. English crowds saw him for the first time in 1933, and those at Old Trafford for the second Test appreciated what all the fuss was about when he played a superb innings of 169 not out. When England toured the Caribbean again in 1934/35, it was not until the final Test in Kingston that he really made the bowlers pay. That was when he compiled his highest Test score of 270 not out to clinch the West Indies' first series win.

Headley had the distinction of a hundred in each innings at Lord's in

1939 although, perversely, that was the Test that the West Indies lost on that tour. After the War, he was honoured to be named as the first black captain of the West Indies. It was after the first innings that his back became too painful for him to continue, so he batted at 11 in the second innings. He played one Test in India in 1948 before injury struck again, but was recalled at the age of 44 to take on England in 1954. He did not contribute greatly to a West Indian triumph by 140 runs, and bowed out of the game.

Headley had achieved so much during his glittering career. It has been said that the West Indian tradition of great batsmen was founded on his outstanding performances. His success was all the greater because, at the time, he was carrying West Indian cricket on his shoulders, hence his nickname of "Atlas". But he discharged his responsibilities without ever giving a hint of being burdened, and he did so with the greatest style and grace.

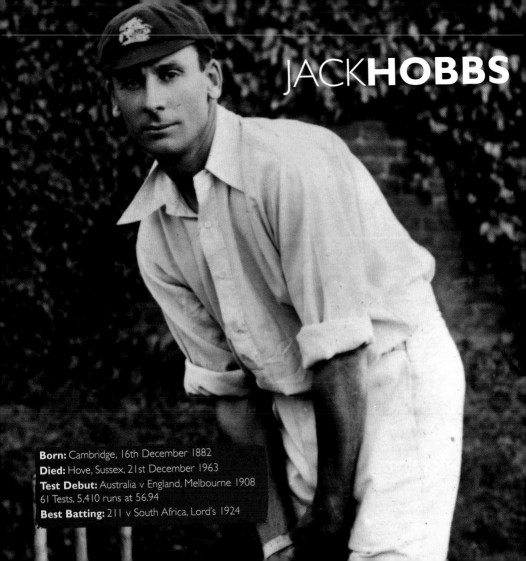

JACK**HOBBS**

Born: Cambridge, 16th December 1882
Died: Hove, Sussex, 21st December 1963
Test Debut: Australia v England, Melbourne 1908
61 Tests, 5,410 runs at 56.94
Best Batting: 211 v South Africa, Lord's 1924

**When John Berry Hobbs was the first professional cricketer to be knighted in 1953
and thus became Sir Jack Hobbs, there was not a voice raised in criticism of the
honour even though the amateur/professional divide was still very much in
evidence. Hobbs' supremacy as a batsman had earned him another title much
earlier in his career – "The Master" – and while he might have been every inch a
professional, it was his demeanour as a gentleman that endeared him to all.**

The man who rose to the very top of the game had humble beginnings. The eldest son
in a large family, his father was the groundsman and umpire at Jesus College, Cambridge.
In fact, it was for the Choir of Jesus College that Hobbs first batted, having practiced with
college servants using a cricket stump and tennis ball, with a net post as a wicket on a
hard tennis court. He did not receive any formal coaching, but his natural eye/hand co-
ordination and ability to learn by watching his peers enabled him to become peerless.

In his first-class career with Surrey and England he scored 61,237 runs with 197
centuries. He would undoubtedly have made more but for the intrusion of the Great War.
He was 36 when cricket resumed after the conflict, yet 132 of his hundreds were still to be
recorded. Hobbs himself did not pay much attention to records and statistics. He was
known to give his wicket away once he had reached three figures to give others a chance,
unless it was important to the team for him to stay there. And he did not rate his post-war
runs as highly as those scored earlier, because "they were nearly all made off the back foot."

He arrived at the Oval only after Essex had spurned the opportunity to look at the young
man playing on their doorstep. Given a trial by Surrey, he made an immediate impression,
but had to serve a two-year qualifying period. Some of that time he spent playing as a
professional for Cambridgeshire before making his first-class debut for Surrey on Easter
Monday, 1905 against a Gentlemen of England XI captained by W.G. Grace. Hobbs scored
18 and a rapid 88, leading the Doctor to observe: "He's going to be a good'un."

His second match was, ironically, against Essex when he made 155 on his
Championship debut and was promptly presented with his county cap. After three
seasons of county cricket he stepped up a level on the 1907/08 tour to Australia, marking
his debut with an innings of 83 in the second Test in Melbourne.

It might have been thought that such a talent would soon be recording Test centuries
by the score. Yet it was not until his 23rd innings that Hobbs reached three figures for the
first time. It came on the mat in South Africa, when he concluded a series in which he

averaged 67.37 (more than double any other English batsman) with an innings of 187 in Cape Town.

Hobbs had such good footwork that he could cope as well with the South African leg-spin and googly bowlers on viciously turning matting wickets as he could with seamers on green wickets in England, the fastest bowlers of the day on quick pitches in Australia, or all types of bowler on rain-affected pitches anywhere in the world. He was the master batsman. Nor was it just a case of stroking the ball to the boundary. Such was his control that if heavy scoring was not possible, he could hit the ball directly to a fielder, but slowly enough to take an easy single.

As a fielder himself, Hobbs became one of the best cover points the game has seen. On the tour of Australia in 1911/12, he was reckoned to have run out no fewer than 15 batsmen with his own hand. In his early days he had ability with the ball, his medium-pace bowling taking 108 first-class wickets at a shade over 25 apiece. But it was as a batsman that he set record after record.

More runs than anyone else, more centuries, more times scoring over 2,000 runs in a season, and he shared in 166 partnerships of 100 or more.

Hobbs was the bridge between what was termed the golden age of batting and the modern era. His career was the thread that bound the fabric of the English game together during that period. His debut was made against W.G. Grace, while his final first-class match, at the age of 51, saw him captaining the Players against the Gentlemen with the likes of Wally Hammond and Les Ames in his side. He recorded his final hundred that season, for Surrey at a freezing Old Trafford against Lancashire and followed it up with 51 not out in the second innings. He stroked the ball about with ease while most other batsmen found the conditions most testing. It summed up Hobbs' career; he began by playing for Jesus and ended batting like God.

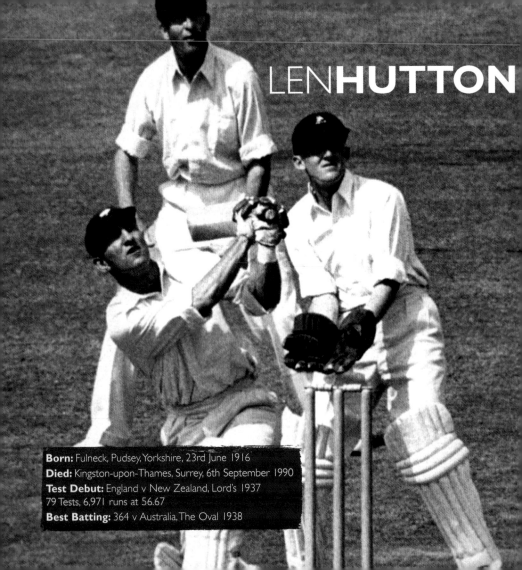

LEN**HUTTON**

Born: Fulneck, Pudsey, Yorkshire, 23rd June 1916
Died: Kingston-upon-Thames, Surrey, 6th September 1990
Test Debut: England v New Zealand, Lord's 1937
79 Tests, 6,971 runs at 56.67
Best Batting: 364 v Australia, The Oval 1938

Not all Sir Leonard Hutton's greatest achievements are easy to put into present day context. He was the first professional regularly to captain England, and to be elected to the MCC while still playing, he set a world record for the highest individual Test innings that stood for a generation, and was knighted following retirement. The easiest, for sure, is the record most coveted by batsmen, since surpassed by two others in this book. Another, Jack Hobbs, was the only previous cricketer to be knighted, and that honourable list now extends well into double figures. The point is that in his time, Hutton was peerless.

He was playing first-class cricket as a teenager. In 1934, his first season, he scored 196 against Worcestershire before showing early signs of skill in adverse batting conditions, making 67 in four hours at Scarborough. The floodgates opened in 1937, the year in which Hutton made his debut for England, against New Zealand at Lord's. Although he avoided a pair only by the narrowest of margins, his class was apparent in the next game at Old Trafford, where he scored his first Test century. To add to his batting, he was a good close fielder and capable of taking useful wickets with leg-spin.

Already he was marked out as a batsman of considerable style and varied strokeplay, capable of tailoring his approach to any given situation. He also possessed huge powers of concentration, never displayed to better effect than the following summer when England went into the final Ashes Test needing a win to square the series. Hutton's 364, which broke Wally Hammond's individual Test record of 336 not out, took more than 13 hours and 847 balls, and by the time he was dismissed the total was 770. Hammond eventually declared on 903 for seven and Australia, with neither Don Bradman nor Jack Fingleton fit to bat, lost by an innings and 579 runs.

Two more big hundreds followed against the West Indies the next season before, with the cricket world apparently at Hutton's feet, the Second World War deprived him of six of his best years. It also left a physical scar, as he required three bone grafts on his left arm after an accident in a gym during commando training. The arm was left weaker and around two inches shorter than the other. Nonetheless, by the time Test cricket resumed, he was ready to feature in a steady England revival.

Hutton excelled in Australia in 1946/7, which caused general bemusement when he was dropped after two Tests (he made 77 in the first) of the 1948 series against Bradman's "Invincibles". Recalled for the fourth, he highlighted the selectors' folly with

innings of 81, 57, 30 and 64. His best season in England followed; in 1949 he scored 3,429 first-class runs at an average of 68, again dipping the bread at the Oval with 206 against New Zealand. Another double followed there against Ramadhin and Valentine the following year, and England's somewhat insipid batting rested almost entirely on Hutton's shoulders (average 88.83) as they were beaten 4-1 Down Under.

But several of Hutton's finest hours were still to come. First appointed captain for the 1952 series against India (despite never having led Yorkshire, as the county maintained the amateur captain tradition) he led England to their Coronation Year Ashes triumph the following summer, in which he was by a distance the best batsman on either side. For pure artistry, the 145 he made at Lord's in that series was regarded as one of the finest innings he ever played.

After a disastrous start in the Caribbean the following winter, it was Hutton who revived England, with 169 and 205 in the third and fifth Tests to square the rubber.

Despite occasional bouts of ill health, he still had another tour in him, to Australia in 1954/5. Although his batting energy had dwindled, Hutton's one half century of the series – 80 in the fourth Test at Adelaide – paved the way for a 3-1 lead, and ensured that the efforts of three youngsters – Peter May, Colin Cowdrey and above all Frank Tyson – did not go to waste. England retained the Ashes, and Hutton ended his career against Australia with nearly 2,500 runs and an average 54.46. When he retired a year later he had captained England 23 times – then a record – without losing a rubber.

In retirement, Hutton pursued a successful business career and did a stint as an England selector, as well as writing regularly about the game he had adorned. He fathered a Yorkshire and England player in Richard, whose son Ben continued the family tradition, not with Yorkshire but Middlesex, where he was to be captain. Few names in English cricket bear the hallmark of such pedigree.

ABOVE
Len Hutton is congratulated by Bill Brown on breaking Don Bradman's record during the 1938 Oval Test. Hutton went on to score 364.

FAR LEFT
Len Hutton strides out at the Oval to open the batting for England against Australia with Bill Edrich in 1938.

IMRAN
KHAN

Born: Lahore, Punjab, 25th November 1952
Test Debut: England v Pakistan, Edgbaston 1971
88 Tests, 3,807 runs at 37.69, 362 wickets at 22.81
Best Batting: 136 v Australia, Adelaide 1990
Best Bowlng: 8/58 v Sri Lanka, Lahore 1982

A wonderfully lithe fast bowler and consistently improving batsman, Imran Khan was undoubtedly the greatest all-round cricketer to play for Pakistan. Add his natural fielding brilliance, particularly in the deep, outstanding captaincy and film-star looks, and you could perhaps term him the real McCoy. The climax of his career – the World Cup victory for his young Pakistan team in 1992 – was the stuff of legends, worthy reward for a distinguished period of leadership in which he managed to instil collective pride in a talented, but too often volatile and disparate unit.

Imran had impeccable cricketing pedigree and connections. Two other Pakistan captains – Majid Khan and Javed Burki – were cousins. He won three blues at Oxford University, one as captain, by which time he had already made his Test debut aged just 18. After two undistinguished tours of England, he broke through as a bowler in Sydney in 1977, taking six wickets in each innings as Greg Chappell's Australians were beaten by eight wickets. His performances on that tour contributed greatly to Pakistan gaining their first Test win on Australian soil, and ensured a one-all draw in the series.

A move from Worcestershire to Sussex followed, along with two winters playing for Kerry Packer's World Series Cricket, as Imran's batting improved from useful to influential. His first Test century came on his home ground of the Gaddafi Stadium in Lahore, rescuing Pakistan against a West Indies attack including Sylvester Clarke, Colin Croft, Malcolm Marshall and Joel Garner. It was an early sign that the great fast bowler could take it as well as dish it out. The following year he excelled in both disciplines in Australia although Pakistan lost the series, before achieving his best Test figures of 8/58 against Sri Lanka back in Lahore.

Imran led Pakistan for the first time on the tour of England in 1982. Although it was a personal triumph (212 runs and 21 wickets in three Tests) Pakistan narrowly

BELOW

Imran Khan bowls Pakistan to victory in the Lord's Test of 1985.

lost an engaging rubber 2-1. No such reversals followed in the ensuing home series against Australia and India, in which Pakistan – and Imran – carried all before them. They won both 3-0 and in the third Test against India at Faisalabad, Imran achieved the astonishing feat of taking 11 wickets in the match for the second successive time, adding a first innings 117 for good measure.

None of the four great all-rounders of his era, apart perhaps from Sir Richard Hadlee, improved as much as Imran during the last decade of his career. In 51 Tests he averaged a stunning 50 with the bat and 19 with the ball, despite being unable to bowl for nearly three years due to a stress fracture of the shin. Perhaps he was inspired by the captaincy; in his 48 Tests leading Pakistan the batting average rose to 52. Highlights included 21 wickets in Pakistan's victorious series in England in 1987 (and 118 in the final Test at the Oval) and, more significantly, 23 wickets in the Caribbean the following winter as Pakistan came within a whisker of beating the all-powerful West Indies.

Imran described Pakistan's victory in the fifth World Cup in Australia in 1992 as "the most thrilling and satisfying cricket moment of my life". In the floodlit final at the MCG,

they beat England by 22 runs after Imran, in his 40th year and with a troublesome right shoulder, had urged his team to imitate the action of the cornered tiger. Knowing that all four previous finals had been won by the side batting first, Imran chose to do so upon winning the toss, and his innings of 72, batting at number three, was the highest and most influential of the match. England's reply never gathered momentum, and it was Imran himself who sealed Pakistan's triumph with his final ball in international cricket.

Imran dedicated the victory to the cause of the cancer hospital he had founded in Lahore in memory of his mother, Shaukat Burki, who had died of the disease seven years earlier. Even though some of the most ardent England supporters were amongst those hoping he might manage one final tour the following summer, there could hardly have been a more appropriate moment to retire from the game he had graced so comprehensively over two decades.

Involvement with politics in Pakistan followed, as well as a high-profile, though ultimately unsuccessful, marriage to Jemima Goldsmith, heiress to a famous Anglo-French financier. But the shining, abiding memory of Imran Khan will surely be for his prowess on the cricket field where, Sir Garfield Sobers apart, he was one of the greatest all-rounders ever seen.

FAR LEFT
Another victim for Imran.

MIDDLE
Imran has taken the final English wicket to win the World Cup for Pakistan in Melbourne in 1992.

BELOW
The captain shows off the spoils of the World Cup final success in 1992.

ALAN
KNOTT

Born: Belvedere, Kent, 9th April 1946
Test Debut: England v Pakistan, Trent Bridge 1967
95 Tests, 4,389 runs at 32.75
269 dismissals (250 caught, 19 stumped)
Best Batting: 135 v Australia, Trent Bridge 1977

When he retired from first-class cricket in 1985, Alan Knott was hailed by Mike Brearley, his latter-day England captain, as a genius. Brearley was referring not only to Knott's wicket-keeping, an art in which he was peerless in his time and arguably ever since, but also to his batting, which was both audacious and increasingly unorthodox. Never more dangerous than in a crisis, he rescued numerous England innings with verve and bravado, at times batting, as John Woodcock put it, "with the effrontery of a bandit".

Alan Philip Eric Knott was heir to a glittering Kent tradition. Les Ames and Godfrey Evans had sparkled for England before him; Paul Downton (after moving to Middlesex) and Geraint Jones were to graduate later. By 1967, aged just 21, Knott was taking seven catches on his England debut. Evidence of his versatility with the bat came on his first tour, to the Caribbean, when he made 73 in four hours at Georgetown to help his captain and Kent team-mate, Colin Cowdrey, secure the famous draw that enabled England to win the series. Knott used his feet superbly against spin, a trait that would be apparent in later years against India.

As a 'keeper, his finest period standing up came early while he established his legendary partnership for Kent and England with Derek Underwood. It was off "Deadly" that Knott took his greatest Test catch (pictured left), from a slower ball edged by India's Dilip Sardesai and held, one-handed at full stretch, at the Oval in 1971. Standing back, as was often his preference, he was stupendous. His judgement on whether and when to go for the ball was unerring; time and again he dived in front of slip to take a catch of breathtaking brilliance. The bowlers, including Geoff Arnold who provided him with more victims than any other, stood and applauded.

Nevertheless, it was fitting that it was off Underwood that Knott stumped Lawrence Rowe of the West Indies in 1976, again at the Oval, to break Evans' world record for Test dismissals. There were more dazzling moments to follow, including a diving, leg side catch to dismiss his great Australian rival Rod Marsh in Ian Botham's first Test in 1977. And amongst those watching the reflex, one-handed effort off Tony Greig that dismissed Rick McCosker that same summer was a strip of a lad from Stroud in Gloucestershire. Jack Russell decided then and there to learn and master the same art.

As a batsman, Knott's favoured strokes were the cut and the sweep, which he played on length, not line, although he could belt the ball over midwicket (to Jeff Thomson's

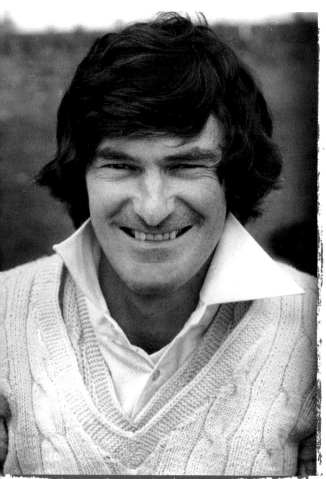

consternation, Knott once hit him for an enormous six there) and he possessed a cultivated, if rarely employed cover drive. Three innings stand out. At Edgbaston in 1971, England were 127 for five in reply to Pakistan's 608. "He really is going berserk," observed commentator Peter West as Knott blazed a two-hour century. At Adelaide in 1975 he made an unbeaten 106 against Lillee and Thomson at their fiercest, adapting to the challenge by repeatedly upper-cutting the ball over the slips.

But his best Test innings came at Trent Bridge against Australia in 1977. He arrived at 82 for five to join Geoff Boycott, who had just run out the local hero Derek Randall. By the time he was out for 135 (Boycott also made a century), Knott had transformed a losing position into a winning one. By then he had joined World Series Cricket, allowing his rival Bob Taylor to flourish for England. But Knott was recalled, largely at Brearley's behest, in 1981 when he followed a scintillating half-century at Old Trafford with a match-saving one in his final Test at the Oval.

Knott was a cricketer of foibles. In the early part of his career he touched the bails at the start of an innings, not out of superstition, he claimed, but to make sure they were properly in place. He had a routine of bending and stretching exercises between deliveries, which caused irritation to some but were simply a means of keeping a naturally stiff body supple. He was chary of drafts, keeping his collar up and sleeves down on the field and donning numerous sweaters off it, even in India. He was fastidious about what he ate and meticulous in his match preparation. All of this was born of utter professionalism.

A devoted family man, Knott did a spell as England's wicket-keeping coach in retirement, but emigrated to Cyprus after the job was no longer deemed full-time. Since then he has been largely absent from the game he so invigorated. But to a generation of cricket lovers who grew up watching his feline grace behind the stumps and wonderful ability to improvise in front of them, the memories are imperishable.

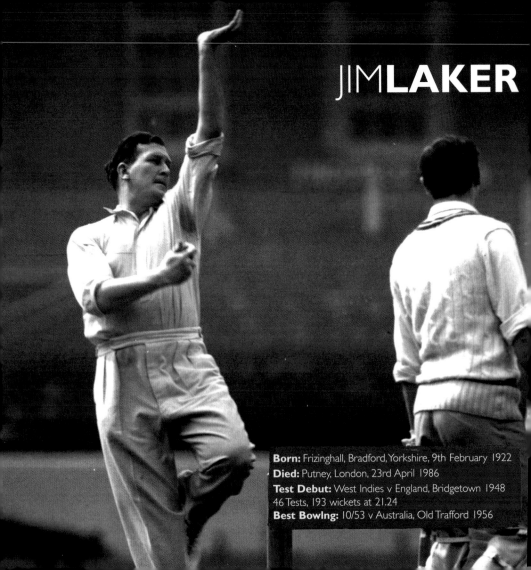

JIM**LAKER**

Born: Frizinghall, Bradford, Yorkshire, 9th February 1922
Died: Putney, London, 23rd April 1986
Test Debut: West Indies v England, Bridgetown 1948
46 Tests, 193 wickets at 21.24
Best Bowlng: 10/53 v Australia, Old Trafford 1956

After Jim Laker had taken 19 Australian wickets in the 1956 Old Trafford Test, his spinning partner Tony Lock was asked if he felt bad about taking the one wicket that prevented Laker from claiming all 20 in the match. Lock is reported to have replied that Laker had taken 19 to prevent him getting all 20 himself.

BELOW
Jim Laker – after his playing days.

It is highly unlikely that anyone will ever do better in a Test, which is enough in itself to give Laker his place in cricket's Pantheon. To take all ten wickets in a Test innings is an outstanding feat in itself; only Anil Kumble has matched that. But to achieve such an analysis in the second innings after taking nine wickets in the first is simply the stuff of legends.

James Charles Laker was 24 when he made his first-class debut for Surrey in 1946. Playing against a formidable Combined Services side, he made an immediate impression with three wickets in each innings with his crafted, highly-spun off-breaks. Later in the season he took his first wicket in an inter-county match at Kingston-upon-Thames, when the unfortunate Rodney Exton of Hampshire was caught between the knees of Alf Gover in the gully as the fielder was pulling his sweater over his head. Laker was not to require such good fortune to take his other 1,943 first-class wickets.

1956 was a vintage year for Laker. He played against the Australians on no fewer than seven occasions, taking the little matter of 63 wickets at a mere ten runs apiece. 46 came in the Tests. Playing for Surrey against the tourists at the Oval before his 19 for 90 match analysis at Old Trafford, he took 10 for 88 in the first innings.

After his early matches for Surrey, he was taken on to the Oval staff in 1947 and the following winter he made his England debut in Barbados. It was quite an entry into Test cricket with seven for 103 from 37 overs. Despite that performance, and returning the remarkable figures of 14-12-2-8 in the 1950 Test trial in his home town of Bradford, he was not at first a regular in the England team.

1950 was his best summer with 166 wickets as Surrey made the County Championship their own property with eight titles in nine seasons. Perhaps that first success in the sequence owed more than a little to the fact that Laker played in only one Test that summer. He was in and out of the England team until his annus mirabilis of 1956, when weight of wickets at the highest level demanded his inclusion in the national side.

Laker had the ideal temperament for a spin bowler. Calm and unruffled, he bowled with the type of action that made you wonder why anyone should attempt to bowl off-breaks any other way. He rarely got excited, and even when he took those 19 Australian wickets at Old Trafford with the ball turning sharply off a rain-affected pitch, each success was acknowledged by a shy smile and a hitch of the trousers. Even when he took his tenth wicket in the second innings, there was no hysterical mobbing and hugging. A simple handshake from colleagues, a look on his face that said he had done a good job, and off he strolled towards the pavilion.

On a pitch like that offering help, Laker's great accuracy came to the fore. It meant that he kept pressure on the batsmen the whole time, while close catchers had the confidence to go really close in the days before helmets and the rest of the fielders' armour.

Ted Dexter played one Test with Laker and remembers fielding at short leg. When a new batsman came in, he did not receive the fast dart that off-spinners so often deliver in the modern game. Instead,

The Little Book of **CRICKET** LEGENDS

as Dexter crouched down, a perfectly flighted delivery came audibly fizzing through the air while the poor batsman tried to make up his mind whether to go forward or back as his eyes went ever further up to follow the trajectory of the ball. It represented a thorough mastery of the finger spinner's art.

That match in Melbourne in 1959 was Laker's last for England. He left Surrey that year, wrote a book which caused much offence among the authorities, but was persuaded by former England colleague Trevor Bailey to play three more seasons of county cricket with Essex. They were successful years, despite the propensity for green, seamer-friendly wickets in his new county. On one occasion at Romford, Bailey asked Laker to go out before the toss to give his assessment of the pitch. Laker wandered out towards the middle and came back some time later. "What do you think of it?" Bailey asked him on his return to the pavilion. "Couldn't find it," was the reply, delivered with the laconic wit that marked his television commentaries in the years following retirement from the game.

FAR LEFT
A study in poise as Laker goes round the wicket.

LEFT
Another perfect ten for Laker, playing for Surrey against the Australians in 1956.

BRIAN**LARA**

Born: Cantaro, Santa Cruz, Trinidad, 2nd May 1969
Test Debut: Pakistan v West Indies, Lahore 1990
121 Tests by the end of 2005, 11,204 runs at 53.86
Best Batting: 400* v England, Antigua 2004

Amongst all of cricket's myriad statistics, a unique distinction is held by Brian Lara. He is the only man to reclaim the world individual Test batting record. Add to that his current status as Test cricket's leading run scorer, and you already have a fair measure of the man's achievement. It is the more telling given the era in which he played, as the West Indies slipped from the great heights they reached in the 1980s. How Lara may have wished, since the turn of the Millennium, for a bowling attack of the quality once commanded by Clive Lloyd. In three spells as West Indies captain, he has had a far trickier furrow to plough.

It was more than three years before shooting to international stardom that Brian Charles Lara made his Test debut in 1990, in a West Indies batting line-up still headed by Greenidge and Haynes. Opportunities were limited until 1992/93 when Lara showed the first evidence of his huge appetite for runs, with 277 at the SCG against Allan Border's Australia. Just five feet five inches tall and left-handed, with a high backlift and a crouch like that of a panther poised to pounce, he was clearly offering something sensational to batsmanship, even by Caribbean standards.

It was back home that Lara confirmed his class the following season, and in doing so drove a suffering England attack to despair. He improved on 83 in the first Test with 167 in the second, but it was in the final match at Antigua that he first etched his name on the list of cricketing immortals. Watched by Sir Garfield Sobers, Lara made 375, ten runs more than the legendary all-rounder's world Test record, set against Pakistan in Jamaica 36 years earlier. The moment when the two players marked the passing of a mantle with a celebratory hug was one of the most moving in recent cricket history.

It carried scarcely less significance when, just seven weeks later, Lara recorded the highest-ever score in first-class cricket, an unbeaten 501 for Warwickshire against Durham at Edgbaston. But his exalted

status, particularly in the modern media age, had not come without constraints. And having broken two such records, where else was he to go? He could not maintain such stupendous standards when Australia toured the Caribbean in 1995, although he again feasted on England's bowling in the drawn rubber that summer. He struggled for most of the ensuing series against Australia, but contributed effectively against India back in the Caribbean. By the time England next visited in 1997/98, he had succeeded Courtney Walsh as captain.

West Indies won that series 3-1, but of more significance to them – and to Lara himself – was the visit of Steve Waugh's dominant Australians in 1998/99. Lara took their bowlers on almost single handed to score 213, 153 not out and 100 in successive Tests. West Indies drew the rubber two-all; without Lara, they would most likely have been pulverised.

But the pressure of leading a team in decline soon told, and he had handed over to Jimmy Adams by the time West Indies were beaten in England in 2000 for the first time since 1969, and lost 5-0 in Australia the following winter. Big hundreds continued to flow, but all too often in a losing cause. Nonetheless Lara was persuaded to undertake a second spell in charge, and

after his Test record was beaten by Australia's Matthew Hayden in 2003, he astounded the cricket world by reclaiming it, again in Antigua against England, at the end of a lean series the following year. His undefeated 400 ensured that the West Indies avoided a series whitewash.

Lara has served West Indies well in one-day internationals, helping them to the World Cup semi-finals in 1996, and leading them, against the odds, to the ICC Champions Trophy in 2004. But when the time comes for him to retire, it is for his Test exploits that he will be venerated. Such has been the pressure that at times he has railed against it. He once claimed that cricket was ruining his life, and later threatened to resign as captain if his team did not play better. But when he passed Allan Border's record of 11,174 Test runs late in 2005, the Australian was amongst the first to pay tribute. "I have had the pleasure of seeing him play a lot of cricket," Border said, "and there is no doubt he is a genuine genius."

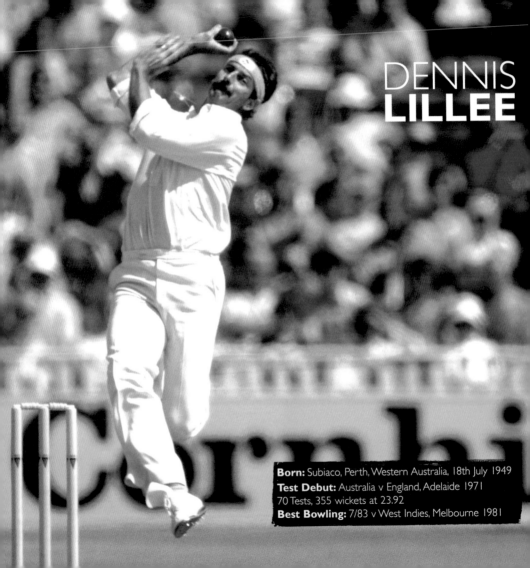

DENNIS
LILLEE

Born: Subiaco, Perth, Western Australia, 18th July 1949
Test Debut: Australia v England, Adelaide 1971
70 Tests, 355 wickets at 23.92
Best Bowling: 7/83 v West Indies, Melbourne 1981

Many claim, with total conviction and no little justification, that Dennis Lillee was the best fast bowler ever. To measure up to such a standard, it would have been necessary to possess all the attributes; Lillee did. At the outset of his career he was the fastest bowler around. When his pace was used more sparingly, following his back injury, he still employed the bouncer and yorker, but had added swing and cut, both ways, and a change of pace.

You had only to see Lillee run in to realise that you were watching a special bowler. It was a purposeful run, full of menace. Leaning forward, he took long strides but maintained perfect balance. His characteristic drooping moustache bristled, the luxuriant dark hair (in his early days!) flopped up and down, a medallion glinted in the sun, while his voluminous shirt billowed in the wind.

The action itself was an incomparable piece of living, moving art. On reaching the delivery stride, he took off in a leap that would get him airborne long enough to turn perfectly sideways while his left arm shot skywards and his front leg pointed at the batsman to give him a lean-back that had him like a coiled spring. Then the trigger was pulled. All the built-up energy was released towards the stumps, or any batsman who happened to intervene. He finished with his head in a perfect position to survey the damage he so often wreaked.

His appeal, which he frequently practiced, involved turning his back on the batsman to implore the umpire with both arms aloft, but all the time continuing his momentum towards the striker's end. Should the batsman be given not out, Lillee was by then close enough to impart some well-chosen words to his intended victim, usually to the effect that the inevitable had been delayed. He would then turn and make his way back towards his mark, perhaps glancing at the umpire as he passed, and flicking perspiration from his forehead with a

BELOW

Like every other facet of his action, Lillee's follow-through was perfect.

The Little Book of **CRICKET** LEGENDS

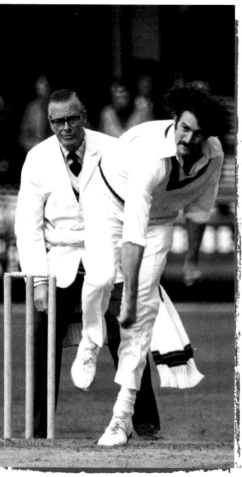

single finger. It was pure theatre.

Dennis Keith Lillee made his first-class debut in 1969 for Western Australia against Queensland in Brisbane, recording the first of what was to become a legendary line in the scorebook: c Marsh b Lillee. It would appear a record 95 times on Test scorecards. He took 32 wickets that season, and the following year represented his state side against the English tourists, but was not included in the Australian team that played the first Test at the WACA a few days later. He had to wait until the circus reached Adelaide before he pulled on his baggy green for the first time. It was also the first time that the Lillee and Thomson partnership appeared in the bowling analysis, but this was Alan Thomson, not Jeff. Without the man who would become half of the most feared opening pair in Test cricket, Lillee still made an impression with figures of five for 84 on his first outing.

When Australia played a four-match series against the Rest of the World the following season, Lillee announced himself as the complete fast bowler with 23 wickets,

including 8 for 29 in a devastating display in Perth, when he bowled out a World XI side that had Sobers batting at seven for 59.

In England in 1972 he took 31 wickets, but in the Caribbean the following February, he played in just one Test before being diagnosed with four stress fractures in his lower back. He spent six weeks in plaster and underwent months of rehabilitation before he was ready to appear in the Test arena again, against the English touring team of 1974/75. England considered it impossible that he could be back to his best, but in partnership with the real Thomson, he destroyed them.

He was lost to World Series Cricket for a time, yet when he came back, he was just as effective, even if he had lost some of his youthful pace and, increasingly, his hair. It was during this phase of his career that he recorded his best Test figures, and in doing so passed Lance Gibbs' record for the most Test wickets – 309. When he retired in 1984, his tally stood at 355.

Lillee was not immune from serious criticism and, perhaps, poor judgement. There was a great furore when he tried to use an aluminium bat against England, and even more controversy when he aimed a kick at Javed Miandad. He was admonished for putting a bet on England (at 500-1) to win the Headingley Test of 1981, yet nobody could accuse him of not trying. He always did.

HOWZAT !

I bat for the
WORLD SERIES

RAY**LINDWALL**

Born: Mascot, Sydney, New South Wales, 3rd October 1921
Died: Greenslopes, Brisbane, Queensland, 23rd June 1996
Test Debut: New Zealand v Australia, Wellington 1946
61 Tests, 228 wickets at 23.03
Best Bowling: 7/38 v India, Adelaide 1948

Ray Lindwall's greatness as a complete fast bowler lies not only in the achievements of his own career. He was the one who restored fast bowling's good name after it was besmirched by the Bodyline controversy, and he was the one who handed the mantle on to the next generation.

BELOW
A portrait of fast-bowler Ray Lindwall in 1953.

He had a wicked bouncer, but delivered it sparingly. Not like the young Alan Davidson, whom he once saw bowl at an opposing tail-ender. Lindwall said that Davidson, with that ball, had admitted that the number eight was a better batsman than he was a bowler. He suggested that he might like to visit the nets to learn to bowl properly, and Lindwall took him along to deliver a lesson.

In early life, Raymond Russell Lindwall played in the streets around his native Sydney. He was said to favour the street along which Bill O'Reilly walked home, just in the hope that he might catch the great leg-spinner's eye. It was duly caught and Lindwall eventually played for O'Reilly's club, St. George, where the great man helped the youngster with his game, using the then novel medium of photography as a coaching aid.

Lindwall was a stickler for practice and developing his game. He had seen Harold Larwood bowl on the infamous 1932/33 tour, and while he found it difficult to accept a Pommie as a hero, he did learn something of how to bowl with a similar physique. While serving with the Australian army in the Pacific during the Second World War, he was physically debilitated by illness yet still marked out his run between palm trees to retain his bowling rhythm.

Home from the war, he was one of seven Australians who made their debuts in the one-off Test in Wellington against New Zealand in 1946. Another debutant was Keith Miller, with whom Lindwall was to form such a dynamic new ball partnership in the years to come, while one of the four returning to Test cricket was none other than Bill O'Reilly.

Lindwall had a quiet match as New Zealand were swept away, despite the honour of taking the first wicket on the resumption of Test cricket, but he did enough to secure a

place in the side to meet England in 1946/47. The first Test in Brisbane saw Lindwall and Miller open the bowling for Australia for the first time. Lindwall had figures of nought for 23 from 12 overs in the first innings, while Miller stole the headlines with seven for 60 from 22.

Lindwall was the quiet, unassuming master of his craft, while Miller was always liable to steal the headlines with a spectacular display. Lindwall did not mind that in the slightest. He was happy to blend in with the background while his partner enjoyed the limelight. He also knew that he had the respect of his fellows and that the pressure he applied could bring rewards at either end.

Lindwall missed the second meeting in Sydney, where Fred Freer took the new ball in his only Test, but was back for the third in Melbourne where he scored the first of his two Test hundreds. He was to be a fixture in the Australian side for the next decade as Lindwall and Miller became one of the legendary fast bowling pairings.

Under six feet tall, with a bowling arm that never reached a classical height, he was nonetheless the complete fast bowler. He was not quite as quick as some

of the other greats of his type, but he was operating under the old back foot no ball law, so by the time he had glided along on his toe end, he was a bit short of the statutory 22 yards. For the batsman, it was like someone bowling at around 90 miles an hour.

Lindwall was primarily an outswing bowler, but added the inswinger for variation. Both deliveries moved as much as anyone has

FAR LEFT
The scorer of two Test centuries did not look best pleased with this dismissal.

LEFT
Ray Lindwall smashes to the boundary for Australia.

ever achieved at his pace. His bouncer, from his low arm, would skid onto the batsman at disconcerting height rather than ballooning over his head. Add to that the yorker and a change of pace, all after a liquid run that made him look as though he was gliding in on casters, and you can understand why he was acknowledged as the master of his art.

Perhaps the most significant thing about Lindwall was his metronomic accuracy. Not many bowlers of his pace have possessed his immaculate control. Early in his career, he realised that relying on catches would not necessarily give him a good return. It was a lesson well learned, because a remarkably high percentage of his wickets were bowled. On the tour of England in 1948, exactly half his 86 wickets fell in that fashion.

He saved some of his best performances for matches against England. At the Oval in 1948, he finished with figures of six for 20 as England were bowled out for 52. But the figures against any opponent reflected the relentless consistency of Lindwall's bowling.

MALCOLM
MARSHALL

Born: Bridgetown, Barbados, 18th April 1958
Died: Bridgetown, Barbados, 4th November 1999
Test Debut: India v West Indies, Bangalore 1978
81 Tests, 376 wickets at 20.94
Best Bowling: 7/22 v England, Old Trafford 1988

When a fast bowler causes batsmen misery and pain, it is difficult to understand how they can like him. Respect him, yes; admire him, without doubt, but to regard him with genuine affection means that he must be a special person. Malcolm Denzil Marshall was accorded that standing, for he was not only one of the game's great fast bowlers but also a thoroughly likeable individual.

When he died at the tragically early age of 41, the universal outpouring of grief was a mark of the esteem in which he was held by colleague and opponent alike. He had a warm personality and a cheerful disposition, yet he also possessed all the weapons that one fast bowler could possibly desire. Ask leading batsmen of his time whom they rated as the best they faced, and with few exceptions they will plump for Marshall.

He was just a little bit different from both his contemporaries and predecessors in the West Indian pace battery that ruled world cricket for a decade. While Joel Garner measured six feet eight inches and the likes of Michael Holding and Colin Croft easily topped six feet, Marshall was no more than five feet eleven. But if he lacked inches, he was blessed with a phenomenally fast arm and, furthermore, dispelled any notion that fast bowlers merely ran in and hurled it down as fast as possible. He was a thinking bowler who happened to be very quick.

His father was killed in a motor accident when he was a baby, so it was his grandfather who taught him the rudiments of the game. His cricketing education advanced as, like most Bajans of his age, he played cricket for hour after hour on the beach, in the road or in clearings in the sugar cane. He was originally a batsman, but as he progressed into club cricket he developed as a bowler before making his debut for Barbados against Jamaica in February 1978. He took six for 77 and, incredible though it may appear, was selected to go to India with the West Indies on the strength of that single first-class match. Caribbean cricket had

BELOW
Australian Graeme Wood was forced to retire hurt after being hit by a Malcolm Marshall bouncer at Headingley in the World Cup in 1983.

been decimated by defections to World Series Cricket, and there were few other candidates with such credentials.

Marshall's fifth first-class match was his Test debut, when he came on first change and took one for 53 from 18 overs. Both his economy and strike rates were to improve dramatically in the years ahead; by the end of his career he had conceded only 2.68 runs per over and taken a wicket every 46.76 balls. And these statistics vary little across all types of cricket – first-class, one-day internationals and domestic limited overs matches. Whenever he crossed the boundary rope, he tried his utmost. He also retained enough of his early batting promise to score ten Test fifties and seven first-class hundreds.

After his meteoric elevation, it took time for him to fulfil his potential. But he had already shown enough for Hampshire to take him on as the successor to another great West Indian fast bowler, Andy Roberts. Marshall's unstinting efforts meant that he was quickly accepted as more than just another hired gun: he became very much part of the family. Not only did he put much in, but he learned from the experience of playing county cricket, completing the education that had been denied him when he was thrust into the international arena so early.

When the Packer players returned, Marshall was used primarily as cover for Roberts, Holding, Croft and Garner.

The Little Book of **CRICKET** LEGENDS

But as they grew older and Marshall improved, he eventually commanded a regular place in the side. In 1982 he took 134 wickets for Hampshire, and when the West Indies entertained India in 1983, Marshall staked his claim to be a first-choice bowler with 21 wickets in the series.

From then on, the sight of his somewhat frenetic run and explosive, if front-on, action became a feature of West Indian cricket. His stock ball was the outswinger, while he was never shy of dropping it short to produce a nasty, skidding bouncer. He developed an inswinger delivered with a scarcely noticeable change of action, and found a devastating leg-cutter.

As an example of his commitment, he broke his thumb while fielding on the first day of the 1984 Headingley Test. Yet when the ninth wicket fell with Larry Gomes approaching a century, Marshall came in with his left arm encased in plaster. He batted long enough for Gomes to reach the milestone, and hit a one-handed four of his own, before taking seven for 53. He missed the fourth Test but was back at the Oval to achieve another five-wicket return, before confirming he was right at the top of his trade with a succession of successful series.

Marshall played on for Hampshire for two years after his retirement from international cricket, and spent some time with Natal where he was inevitably revered. Shortly after becoming coach of the West Indies, he was diagnosed with cancer of the colon. He married his long-time girlfriend Connie just weeks before his death stunned his many friends across the cricketing world.

FAR LEFT
Marshall delivers more distress to England.

MIDDLE
The ramrod straight bowling arm about to deliver.

BELOW
Marshall at the start of his run – a sight feared by all batsmen.

KEITHMILLER

Born: Sunshine, Melbourne, Victoria, 28th November 1919
Died: Mornington Peninsula, Melbourne, Victoria, 11th October 2004
Test Debut: New Zealand v Australia, Wellington 1946
55 Tests, 2,958 runs at 36.97, 170 wickets at 22.97
Best Batting: 147 v West Indies, Jamaica 1955
Best Bowling: 7/60 v England, Brisbane 1946

Keith Miller would have been a legend even if he had never played cricket. He was the sort of man who would have excelled in whatever pursuit he had chosen and the game was fortunate to benefit from his sumptuous gifts. Named, fittingly, after two Australian aviation pioneers, Keith and Ross Smith, he was born and raised in the somewhat staid city of Melbourne, beginning his cricket career with Victoria. It was only after the Second World War that he moved to Sydney and New South Wales, where he could freely express his natural talents.

BELOW

Keith Miller outside
Buckingham Palace,
after receiving an
MBE with fellow-
recipient and
Australian Test
player, Ian Johnson.

During the war he had enlisted in the RAAF, flying Beaufighters and then Mosquito fighter-bombers on raids over Germany. Perhaps that experience shaped his perspective on life and cricket. Once, when asked about the pressures associated with the modern game, he replied: "Pressure is a Messerschmitt up your arse. Playing cricket is not." A classical music enthusiast, he diverted on his way back from a raid to fly over Bonn – Beethoven's birthplace. Or so the story goes; it is often difficult to separate substance from myth when dealing with legends.

What is certain is that before the war he was regarded mainly as a batsman; by the time he returned from the conflict he was one of the most potent all-rounders the game has seen. It was at the end of the war that he emerged as a figure who was likely to dominate world cricket. "Flight Sergeant Miller" and then "Pilot Officer Miller" was receiving very good reviews for his performances with the Australian Services and Dominions teams that played in England before demobilisation.

His Test debut was delayed by the war, but once he could concentrate on cricket in peacetime rather than grabbing games between flying missions, his form demanded his inclusion in Australian teams, even if his cavalier lifestyle did not always endear him to the selectors. For example, after he had featured prominently in the success of Bradman's 1948 "Invincibles", he was left out of the original

party to tour South Africa, although injury did open up a place for him.

It had been rumoured that he never got on with Sir Donald Bradman, because Miller's inherent joie de vivre clashed with The Don's very pragmatic approach to cricket and life. They were totally different, but it did not mean they were sworn enemies. Speaking at Miller's memorial service in 2004, Bradman's son, John, said, "My father told me that he never had a more loyal supporter than Keith Miller. People speak of contrasts, but the similarities go deeper."

Bradman could not resist the opportunity to score runs; Miller could be disinterested if they did not have to be worked for. At Southend in 1948, the Australians rattled up 721 all out – in a day. Bradman top-scored with 187 while Miller was bowled first ball by Trevor Bailey. Bradman, at the non-striker's end, was heard to mutter, "He'll learn." There was some conjecture that Miller wanted no part in such an easy contest and simply lifted his bat out of the way of a straight one, or that he had an assignment back in the team hotel that was altogether more enticing than thrashing a few runs off an already dispirited county attack.

Not for him a life of denial. It is said that he was known to get out of a taxi shortly before the start of play, still resplendent in his dinner jacket from the previous evening's festivities. That was what opposition batsman feared, for when fragile or hung-over, Miller was at his most lethal. A few yards of run, the arm would sweep over in a high arc, and the ball would arrive quicker than

FAR LEFT
Miller in the nets.

LEFT
Miller mayhem.
Entertaining, even
when out for a
duck, caught
Trueman bowled
Laker at the Oval in
1953.

anything else. Or he might come in off his full run and bowl a perfect googly as quickly as it is possible to bowl one.

Whether it was a match-winning spell of explosive fast bowling or a barnstorming innings, Miller was sure to enthral the crowd at some stage in the match. He would have made an excellent captain of his country, but somehow the selectors could never quite bring themselves to make the appointment. Stories abound of his time in charge of New South Wales. Like the time he set the field by telling his fielders to "scatter". Or when they took the field with 12 men. Miller looked round and addressed the other 11 with the words: "One of you had better bugger off."

Despite such apparent levity, he led his state side to three consecutive Sheffield Shield titles. Miller was an inspirational character that players would always follow. He was a fine batsman and an outstanding bowler – one of those genuine all-rounders whose career figures will never convey the élan of the player.

His social life was as hectic as every facet of his existence. It was once written: "Women wanted to be with him, while men wanted to be him." There were rumours of a romantic involvement with Princess Margaret (that he neither confirmed nor denied) but they summed him up as a person. At total ease in the company of princes or paupers. They all loved him.

VIVIAN
RICHARDS

Born: St. John's, Antigua, 17th March 1952
Test Debut: India v West Indies, Bangalore 1974
121 Tests, 8540 runs at 50.23
Best Batting: 291 v England, The Oval 1976

"Funny how Viv tends to get becalmed in the 170s." The words of Eric Hill, then an ever-present in the Taunton press box, as Vivian Richards was taking a comparative breather on the way to the highest score of his first-class career, 322 against Warwickshire, off just 258 deliveries, on an unforgettable, sunlit June day in 1985. His 50 boundaries included eight sixes, one of them drilled so hard and flat in the direction of the same press box that some of the occupants dived for cover.

BELOW
The poise of Viv
Richards in 1980.

Few who saw Richards in his prime would disagree that he was the most awesome batsman of his day; indeed his great friend and contemporary Ian Botham adjured that there has never been a better player. Hawk-eyed, with feline reflexes and a powerful physique, Richards' mere emergence from the pavilion was enough to send the crowd into a ferment of expectation. He never wore a helmet, and his swagger, head tilted slightly skywards, contributed further to his intimidatory demeanour as he approached the crease. The twirl of the bat, the slap on the top of its handle, as if he was coaxing ketchup from a bottle; the unhurried look around the field, the adjustment of his cap; all contributed to the aura, often further enhanced by the disappearance of his first delivery to the boundary.

Although he made an unbeaten 192 in his second Test at Delhi, Isaac Vivian Alexander Richards came of international age in the 1975/76 series against Greg Chappell's Australians. Promoted to open in the last two Tests as Clive Lloyd desperately sought to counter the barrage of Lillee and Thomson, he responded with scores of 30, 101, 50 and 98. By then he had already caught the eye in the field, with three run-outs in the inaugural World Cup final at Lord's in 1975 which contributed enormously to the West Indies' win. He was also under contract to Somerset, a team he helped to one-day glory later in the decade, but which he was ultimately to leave amid much acrimony.

1976 was the year in which Richards, at the age of just 24, set a record that has so far survived even the current proliferation

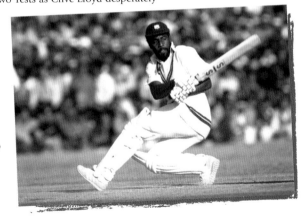

VIVIAN**RICHARDS**

of international cricket. He scored 1,710 runs in the calendar year, at an average of 90 and with seven hundreds, culminating in his 291 on a parched Oval at the end of an unusually arid English summer. Not for the first time or the last, England's bowlers were at a loss as to how to attack him. Further success followed against Pakistan in the Caribbean before he joined Kerry Packer's World Series Cricket.

Lord's, described by Richards as the Mecca of cricket, almost invariably brought out the best in him. After his fielding exploits in 1975, he played a match-winning innings of 138 in the 1979 World Cup final which was followed by an unbelievable running catch at deep midwicket to dismiss Botham. He took the form back into the Test arena with a magical series in Australia before returning to Lord's the following year to make 145. Throughout he showed the wonderfully agile footwork, hand-to-eye co-ordination and ability to improvise which had by now become his hallmark.

Nowhere was this better illustrated than at Old Trafford in 1984, when Richards played what still ranks arguably

The Little Book of **CRICKET** LEGENDS

as the finest one-day international innings. West Indies were apparently without a prayer at 102 for seven but Richards, aided first by Eldine Baptiste and then by Michael Holding, bludgeoned a scintillating, unbeaten 189 off 170 balls. To illustrate the problems faced by England's attack, Neil Foster bowled one delivery of full length just outside the leg stump, only to see Richards take two steps towards square leg before driving it straight for six.

By the time he succeeded Clive Lloyd as Test captain the following year, the West Indies dominated world cricket. Their four-man pace attack was capable of destroying any batting line-up, while Richards remained the star batsman. England were often on the receiving end; in a one-day international at Port of Spain in 1985, he hit a breathtaking 82 off just 39 balls, and six weeks later he played a Test innings on his home ground of St. John's, Antigua, that dazzled even by limited-overs standards. Time and again the arena looked too small for him as seven sixes were deposited into various different stands. Mobbed by his own people on reaching his hundred, his joy was palpable and unalloyed.

Richards retired from Test cricket in 1991, having scored a half-century in all five matches of his final series in England. Borne off the field by his teammates after ensuring they could not lose the rubber in the previous match at Edgbaston, he was saluted by the England team as he walked off for the last time at the Oval. He was later knighted for his services to cricket; no one, in his time or since, can have batted with such majesty.

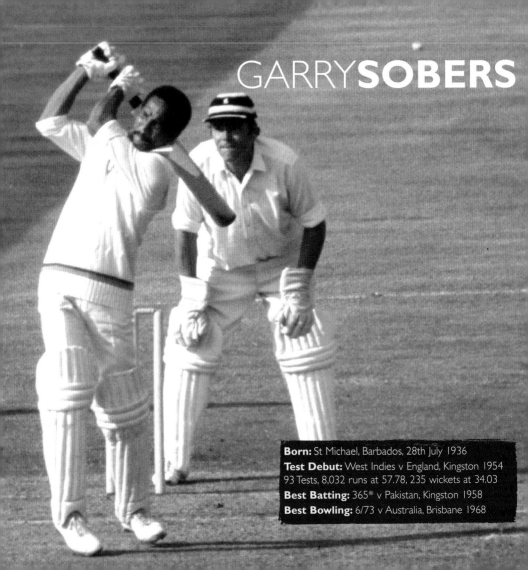

GARRY**SOBERS**

Born: St Michael, Barbados, 28th July 1936
Test Debut: West Indies v England, Kingston 1954
93 Tests, 8,032 runs at 57.78, 235 wickets at 34.03
Best Batting: 365* v Pakistan, Kingston 1958
Best Bowling: 6/73 v Australia, Brisbane 1968

Her Majesty Queen Elizabeth II reigns over Barbados, but the undeniable king of the island is Garry Sobers. To this day he can walk into a restaurant and other diners will rise to applaud him to his table. His fame is the result of being one of the most versatile cricketers ever seen in the game.

Versatility can sometimes be a cloak to hide deficiencies in the basic elements of cricket. That was not the case with Garfield St. Aubern Sobers, who excelled in all departments. It was Trevor Bailey, knowing a thing or two about the job as one of England's finest, who defined an all-rounder as someone who could command his place in the side as either a batsman or a bowler. Sobers transcended that simple definition. He could most certainly have walked into any team as a batsman alone, but he was also a top-class bowler in three styles, and he possessed a rare ability as a fielder. He was the complete all-rounder by Bailey's or anybody else's definition.

Sobers was born with an extra finger on each hand; they were amputated when he was very young. His father, a seaman, lost his life in the Second World War, so Sobers' boyhood was spent in humble surroundings. He was an all-round sportsman as well as a cricketer, playing football, golf and basketball for Barbados, but it was at cricket that he was to reach the pinnacle.

After the traditional Bajan upbringing of playing the game anywhere and any time it could be played, Sobers graduated to the Barbados side, making his first-class debut aged 16 as an orthodox left-arm spinner. That was in 1953 against the Indian touring team, when he made seven not out batting at number nine, but more notably took seven wickets in the match, four bowled and three lbw. He bowled straight, even at such a tender age.

The following year he made his Test debut, against an England side in which Bailey was instrumental in his team's success. Sobers took four wickets and again

batted usefully at number nine. He was not to stay there, for a number of promising performances propelled him up the order as his batting blossomed. It flowered fully in 1958, when he played against Pakistan in Jamaica. He not only recorded his first Test century, but also went on to break Len Hutton's record for an individual innings when he made 365 not out.

When Frank Worrell gave up the captaincy of the West Indies after the 1963 tour to England, Sobers was appointed and showed the flair he brought to his batting. He tended to be adventurous, believing that he had the ability to rectify any situation. It did not always work out that way. In 1968 he enlivened a match heading for a draw with a bold declaration that set England 215 to win. There was much displeasure throughout the Caribbean when the West Indies lost by seven wickets, and criticism was not deflected by Sobers' heroic efforts to square the series in the final match. There were still mutterings of discontent despite his innings of 152 and 95 not out, along with 68 overs that produced six wickets. England hung on to their last wicket to secure the draw and the series.

Sobers' outstanding personal form against England attracted offers from county clubs and in 1968, he accepted the captaincy of

Nottinghamshire. In his first season, he wrote yet another chapter in the record books by hitting six sixes in an over, bowled by the unfortunate Malcolm Nash of Glamorgan. He also appeared for South Australia where his influence was just as great. He was the only man to do the double of 1,000 runs and 50 wickets in a Sheffield Shield season, and he did it twice.

Perhaps Sobers' greatest innings came in Melbourne in 1972 when he was captaining a Rest of the World XI against an Australian attack spearheaded by Dennis Lillee at his most lethal. Sobers played majestically to reach 254 in the second innings (he was out for a duck in the first) to win a nod of approval from none other than Sir Donald Bradman. He described it as the finest innings he had ever seen.

Everything about Sobers' cricket was both individual and exhilarating. Even the way he walked, with long strides and a certain give in the knee, was imitated by schoolboys everywhere. But it was the fluidity of his batting, with a high backlift and an extravagant follow-through, which made him special. And his extraordinary ability with the ball; it was not unknown for him to bowl in his three differing styles in one session of play. And his fielding, either patrolling the covers with feline grace or lurking at short leg where some of his catches appeared to be the product of a conjurer's trick. When the Queen visited Barbados in 1975, she took the opportunity to dub Sobers "Sir Garfield" on his own territory.

ABOVE

Sobers with the trophy after leading the Rest of the World side to victory over England in 1970.

MIDDLE

Sobers catches Brian Luckhurst of England in the slips at Lord's in 1973.

FAR LEFT

Sobers resplendent in his West Indies blazer at the Oval.

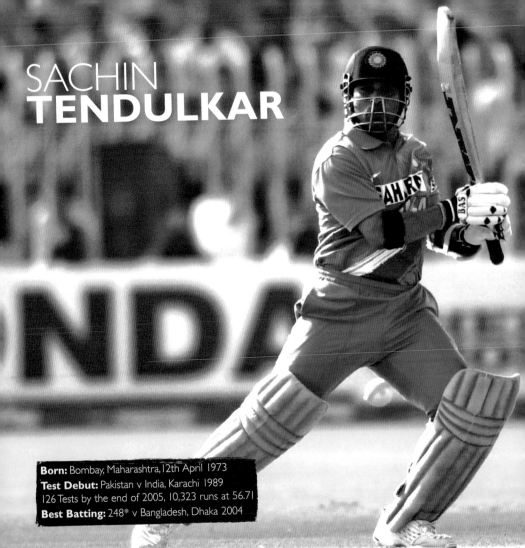

SACHIN
TENDULKAR

Born: Bombay, Maharashtra, 12th April 1973

Test Debut: Pakistan v India, Karachi 1989

126 Tests by the end of 2005, 10,323 runs at 56.71

Best Batting: 248* v Bangladesh, Dhaka 2004

It is a fair assumption that by the end of his career Sachin Tendulkar, after being one of the youngest players to make his Test debut, will have scored more Test runs than anyone else. If accomplished, such status will owe less to logic than to the utter dedication, physical and mental, that India's ultimate superstar has vested in his cricket since before he was a teenager. A scarcely less notable achievement is that he has remained unspoilt by his almost god-like fame or considerable fortune in this media-dominated age.

By the age of ten, Sachin Ramesh Tendulkar was batting on the bumpy lanes of Bandra near his home with a bat not dissimilar to him in stature. At 12, he was scoring a hundred for his school in the Harris Shield. The following year he made nine centuries (including two doubles) to reach 2,336 runs in total. He came under the tutelage of coach Ramakant Achrekar, who used to put a rupee on top of Tendulkar's stumps, saying: "Anyone who gets him out will take this coin. If no one gets him out, Sachin is going to take it." Although he lost a couple, Tendulkar still keeps 13 of the rupees.

He was practicing for a couple of hours every morning and evening, and playing a match in between. For barely a handful of cricketers can the maxim "practice makes perfect" have been as applicable. He flirted with bowling fast, but although he later became a useful bowler of varied disciplines, particularly in one-day cricket, he ultimately heeded the advice to make batting his forte. The results were increasingly stellar. In 1987/8, along the way to 3,000 runs, he established a world-record partnership of 664 with his school friend Vinod Kambli, which placed him firmly in the national consciousness.

Despite Achrekar's fear that he was being pushed too quickly, Tendulkar made his first-class debut for Bombay the following season aged 15, and his century in that game must have allayed the concerns. Nor was there any evidence that the predominantly bottom-hand grip,

BELOW
Sachin Tendulkar is congratulated on his 119 not out against England at Old Trafford in 1990.

attributable to his use of heavy bats in earlier youth, was inconveniencing him. His broadening mental strength, acquired from a depth of preparation that belied his youth, was also a key factor. He averaged a shade below 55 in 11 innings, and his rise to the game's highest level was plainly going to be completed sooner rather than later.

His Test debut could hardly have come against more hostile opposition, or a more threatening attack. For Pakistan Imran Khan and Wasim Akram were joined by Waqar Younis, also on debut, and the leg-spin wizard Abdul Qadir. Tendulkar made 15 (one short of his tender age) amid a barrage of short-pitched deliveries, one of which hit him on the head. He reached a half-century in the next Test at Sialkot, during which he responded to Wasim Akram's sledging by asking him why a bowler of his class should find it necessary. His maiden Test century against England the following year saved India's bacon at Old Trafford; he was still only 17.

It is impossible to do justice here to the glory that has followed since. 148 not out against Australia at the SCG, ensuring a harsh introduction to Test cricket for Shane Warne, and 118 at Perth in the same series. 122 against England on an uneven Edgbaston wicket in 1996 showed the strength of his technique, before he rattled off 169, again in a losing cause, in Cape Town the same year. He has been a constant thorn in Australia's side, never more so than when he made 126 to help set up the famous 2-1 win over Steve Waugh's team at Madras in 2001. Back at the SCG three years later, he made an unbeaten 241 to ensure that there was no fairy-tale ending to Waugh's Test career. After missing six months with an elbow injury in 2005, he

returned after surgery with a century against Sri Lanka, his 35th hundred to put him on top of the list above his old mentor, Sunil Gavaskar.

Although Tendulkar's experience as India's captain was less productive, he played some of his best cricket – particularly in one-day internationals – after returning to the ranks. In 1998 he scored nearly 2,000 one-day runs, helping India reach nine finals. He remained ever eager to bowl his handy medium-pacers, which have taken well over 100 wickets. Add to that his reliable fielding and instinctive ability to read the game, and you have a peerless player of cricket in both its forms. For Tendulkar himself, a private man despite being India's most public figure, it is deserved reward for giving all he has to the game that is his life.

FRED**TRUEMAN**

Born: Stainton, Yorkshire, 6th February 1931
Test Debut: England v India, Headingley 1952
67 Tests, 307 wickets at 21.57
Best Bowling: 8/31 v India, Old Trafford 1952

To predict in August 1964, when Frederick Sewards Trueman became the first bowler to take 300 Test wickets, that he would drop to 19th on the overall list in little more than two decades, would have tempted ridicule. The fact reflects not on his achievement but on how much more international cricket has been played since his time. When Colin Cowdrey held the slip catch at the Oval, just above his right knee, to dismiss the Australian Neil Hawke, Trueman was saluted not only by the victim (who was the first to shake his hand), but also by his teammates and a grateful nation.

BELOW
Trueman and Cowdrey share congratulations after the bowler's 300th Test wicket.

It was the culmination of a Test career that lacked nothing in spirit, controversy or humour. Five feet, ten inches tall, he had a frame tailor-made for fast bowling, with great strength in his shoulders, arms, back and legs, developed during his days in the mining industry as well as in junior cricket. With a classical action, a menacing scowl and unruly hair, "Fiery Fred" helped reduce India to 0/4 on his Test debut at his home ground of Headingley in 1952, ending the series with 29 wickets. A spell in National Service and brushes with authority on the West Indies tour of 1953/4 restricted his appearances over the next three years, after which he was consistency itself, with a deadly, late out-swinger the foremost weapon in his extensive armoury.

By 1957, when he took 22 wickets against the West Indies, Trueman was developing his legendary partnership with Brian Statham, the accurate Lancastrian who raced him to the 250-wicket mark in Tests. And on a far happier trip to the Caribbean in 1959/60 under the captaincy of Peter May, Trueman again impressed with 21 scalps. By this time he had developed into a useful tail-end batsman, particularly strong on the leg-side and good enough eventually to score three first-class centuries. He was also a specialist leg slip, although the ability to throw with either arm enabled him to field virtually anywhere the situation demanded.

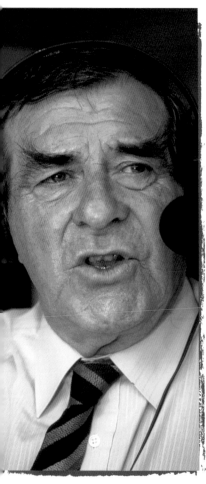

Like many others before and since Trueman, who had begun his Test career as a bowler of raw pace, learned guile as his speed diminished. Against Australia at Headingley in 1961, he took five wickets in 24 balls with his off-cutters without conceding a run as Australia were skittled for 120 in their second innings. He had match figures of 11 for 88 and the old enemy was beaten by eight wickets. At Old Trafford the following year he did almost as well with nine in the match as Pakistan were cast aside by a similar margin. By the time he retired, Trueman had taken 2,304 first-class wickets, an astonishing achievement for a bowler of his type.

In his comments about some players and officials, Trueman was capable of withering bluntness. In his most recent autobiography he described Freddie Brown, his manager on the 1958/59 tour of Australia, as "a snob, bad-mannered, ignorant and a bigot." In an earlier one he wrote of one of his captains at Yorkshire, Vic Wilson: "He didn't smoke or drink. That's fair enough. But he used to stand there sipping orange juice, which I thought was a diabolical shame for a man standing six foot three inches!"

Trueman's aptitude for anecdotes was to reach a wider audience during a lengthy spell with Test Match Special, where he drew productively on his excellent memory, especially during breaks for rain. But he could be over-critical of his fast bowling successors, notably at Old Trafford during the legendary 1981 Ashes series. After a two-over opening onslaught on Bob Willis by Australia's Graeme Wood, Trueman said he would be ashamed to draw his pay

FAR LEFT
Trueman as an expert summariser for Test Match Special in 1997.

LEFT
Fred Trueman takes his 300th Test wicket as Neil Hawke of Australia is caught by Colin Cowdrey at slip at the Oval in 1964.

if he bowled like that in a Test. Willis took three wickets in his next six balls, unwittingly casting the curse of the commentator on his illustrious predecessor.

Notwithstanding such reversals, Trueman's career on and off the field has produced some legendary yarns. When Fred Rumsey, undoubtedly an inferior bowler, had the temerity to bowl him a bouncer, Trueman is alleged to have advanced ominously down the wicket to utter: "Does't tha' want to die, Rumsey?" In retirement, watching footage of the West Indies dispatching him to the boundary five times off consecutive balls, he said: "Isn't it funny how black and white makes you look so much slower?" Some of the stories he simply disclaimed. "I hear things about m'self that I'd never have dreamed in 100 years, and I don't reckon to be short on imagination."

SHANE
WARNE

Born: Ferntree Gully, Victoria, 13th September 1969
Test Debut: Australia v India, Sydney 1992
135 Tests to January 2006, 659 wickets at 25.15
Best Bowling: 8/71 v England, Brisbane 1994

When Shane Warne broke Dennis Lillee's record of 85 Test wickets in a calendar year in 2005, the great fast bowler was there to watch. "There isn't a bit of sadness there for me in passing on the record to the greatest bowler we have seen," Lillee said. It was the crowning moment of a glittering year for the blond Victorian spin king with a penchant for jewellery. Amongst the haul was the mere matter of 40 wickets in the Ashes series, a five-match record, including his 600th in Tests; he is the first bowler to reach the milestone.

Not only has Warne been established as a legend for most of his career, he is widely considered to be the greatest spin bowler ever to set foot on a cricket field. And what a dramatist! From the moment he is handed the ball the effect can be mesmeric. Witness his ambling, unruffled approach to the wicket, the moment of release so often followed by a passionate appeal, and the affronted, prolonged look of injured, angelic innocence should the umpire inexplicably lack the discernment to raise a digit. So strong is Warne's will, you sense that no situation, however unpromising, is necessarily irretrievable.

His story includes enough twists and turns to make Shakespeare dizzy, and not just in the arena itself. What made him special, when he first made his mark, was his novelty. Pace, as purveyed by the all-powerful West Indies, had dominated cricket for more than a decade and Pakistan's Abdul Qadir, a notable exponent of leg spin, had not played Test cricket since 1990. Just when it seemed that the art was in danger of emulating the dodo, Warne rekindled it with a vengeance and a freshness that was utterly spellbinding. And his entry into Test cricket's longest-running drama could simply never have been scripted.

Mike Gatting must be fed up with being asked about it. After all, he has had moments of more acute discomfort, like when he had to fly home from the Caribbean leaving a small piece of his nose embedded in a ball propelled by Malcolm Marshall. But the "Ball of the

Century" was justly so dubbed in 1993. It was Warne's first in Ashes cricket, and while no leggie can expect to pitch it perfectly first up, this one landed outside leg, span in apparent defiance of geometric law and hit the off stump. England's best player of spin was aghast, while the tone was set for a series and a career.

It is just as well for cricket that Warne was not a few inches taller. He wanted to be an Australian Rules footballer. During a brief spell with the Australian Cricket Academy he met the former Australia leg-spinner Terry Jenner, who was to give him invaluable advice throughout his career. Selection for his home state was followed by his Test debut against India in 1992, by which time he was giving the ball a real rip. The Gatting delivery was followed by a career-best eight for 71 against England at Brisbane, and a hat-trick in the next Test of the 1994/95 series, as wickets tumbled to Warne no matter who was batting or where on earth he was bowling.

Drama includes shade as well as light. Numerous stories about Warne's private life culminated in the break-up of his marriage in 2005. He was fined Aus$8,000 in 1995 for accepting money from a bookmaker after talking to him about pitches and weather. To this day, he insists

he did nothing wrong. He was offered, and refused, money to under-perform in a Test by Pakistan's Salim Malik. And a year-long ban from cricket resulted when Warne, after taking a slimming pill offered to him by his mother, tested positive for diuretics. Plainly it sharpened his appetite; he scalped 26 Sri Lankan batsmen in three Tests on his return.

After helping Australia win the 1999 World Cup – he was Man of the Match in the semi-final and final – Warne was denied a last tournament by the ban, imposed after he had already announced his retirement from one-day internationals. The decision was influenced by two major shoulder injuries, and the desire to play Test cricket for as long as possible. So batsmen continue to be caught in his web of intrigue, and bowlers are still piqued by a batsman who has scored more Test runs than anyone without reaching three figures. A strange record that, but then nothing about Shane Warne is run-of-the-mill.

ABOVE
Warne joins captain Steve Waugh with the World Cup in 1999.

MIDDLE
Another step on the way to the World Cup in 1999.

FAR LEFT
Warne in classical batting pose.

The Little Book of **CRICKET** LEGENDS

121

FRANK
WORRELL

Born: Bank Hall, St Michael, Barbados, 1st August 1924
Died: Mona, Kingston, Jamaica, 13th March 1967
Test Debut: West Indies v England, Port of Spain 1948
51 Tests, 3,860 runs at 49.48, 69 wickets at 38.72
Best Batting: 261 v England, Trent Bridge 1950

Frank Mortimer Maglinne Worrell was the sort of cricketer and man who appealed to everyone. For confirmation, consider that the streets of Melbourne were lined in 1961 as his West Indian team left Australia to a ticker-tape farewell. It was an altogether more sombre gathering, but just as heartfelt, when his body was borne home to Barbados after his tragically early death from leukaemia in 1967. That after he had done something unthinkable in those times by moving to Jamaica earlier in his career.

Worrell made a lasting impact in England as well. Westminster Abbey was thronged for the first memorial service to be held for a cricketer there, while the congregation consisted of not only his English and Bajan friends, but also representatives of all West Indian communities in Britain. His great legacy to Caribbean cricket was that he brought all islands together to play as a single entity, and this at a time when a trend towards political independence could have driven them further apart on the cricket field.

Worrell received little or no actual coaching, but developed into a technically correct batsman. So much so that he claimed he could not hit across the line, even when he should have done. Yet it was as a left-arm spinner that he came to prominence in Barbados, making his first-class debut at the age of 18. The first hint that he had the makings of an outstanding batsman came the following season, in 1943, when he was promoted to nightwatchman and carried his bat for 64. By the end of that same season he was opening the innings.

It was not long before he was comfortably established in his batting role, while he developed into a fast-medium bowler rather than a spinner. He combined with John Goddard in 1943/44 to add an unbroken 502 against Trinidad, with Worrell himself making 308. In 1946/47, the Trinidadian bowlers were put to the sword once more as Worrell and Clyde Walcott put on 574 – again undefeated.

It was only a matter of time before he made his Test debut. It came against England in Port of Spain in 1948. The legendary 'Three Ws' of Worrell, Walcott and Weekes, all from Barbados, appeared together on a Test scorecard for the first time, with Worrell coming within three runs of a century in the first innings. He put that failing right in the next Test in Georgetown when he scored 131 not out.

He went to England to play in league cricket in Lancashire, and although he did not tour India with the West Indies in 1948/49, he did go with a Commonwealth XI in 1949/50,

when he gave the first indications of his captaincy skills as well as dominating with the bat. By his first tour of England in 1950 he was an experienced international cricketer, and underlined the fact with his highest Test score. His 261 at Trent Bridge was a masterclass when it came to placement.

Success followed success, and not only with the bat. He took six for 38 against Australia in Adelaide in 1951 and at Headingley in 1957 he took seven English wickets for 70. It was his batting, however, that elevated him to the Pantheon as, in combination with Walcott and Weekes, he gave the West Indian middle order a formidable potential.

Yet even that was not Worrell's greatest contribution to Caribbean cricket. George Headley had one match as the first black captain of the West Indies, but it was to Worrell that the honour of destroying the stigma fell. He was by no means a universally acclaimed choice to take the side to Australia for the 1960/61 tour, but by the end of it

he was acknowledged as an outstanding and much-admired leader.

For the first time, a West Indian team became just that. No longer a collection of Bajans, Jamaicans, Trinidadians or whatever; island loyalties were set aside for the common good. Worrell instilled a strong code of discipline that gave the team self-respect and gained the respect of others.

He imposed himself with the coolest of heads when the series started with the tied Test in Brisbane. All that separated the two sides by the time they got to Melbourne for the fifth Test was two tail-end Australian wickets. The West Indies lost, but had won enormous regard and revitalised what had been a flagging interest in the game in Australia. Ever since, West Indies and Australia have competed for the Frank Worrell Trophy.

With the likes of Garry Sobers, Rohan Kanhai, Lance Gibbs, Wes Hall and Charlie Griffith in the side for his final tour of England in 1963, Worrell had at his command a unit that was worthy of a 3-1 series victory to establish the West Indies as a power in world cricket.

Worrell had studied in Manchester and, following retirement at the end of that 1963 tour, he took up the post of Warden of the University College of the West Indies in Jamaica, and became a senator in the Jamaican Parliament. Knighted in 1964, he seemed destined to play a major role in Caribbean affairs, if not on an even grander stage, before his sudden and most untimely death at the age of 42.

The Little Book of
GRAND PRIX
L E G E N D S
PHILIP**RABY**

The Little Book of
FOOTBALL
L E G E N D S
GRAHAM**BETTS**

The Little Book of
GOLF
L E G E N D S
NEIL**TAPPIN**

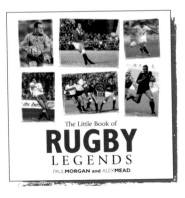

The Little Book of
RUGBY
L E G E N D S
PAUL**MORGAN** and ALEX**MEAD**

THE PICTURES IN THIS BOOK WERE PROVIDED COURTESY OF THE FOLLOWING:

GETTY**IMAGES**
101 Bayham Street, London NW1 0AG

EMPICS
www.empics.com

Concept, Original Design and Art Direction:
VANESSA **and** KEVIN**GARDNER**

Design and Artwork: ADDISON**DESIGN**LTD

Image research: ELLIE**CHARLESTON**

PUBLISHED BY GREEN UMBRELLA PUBLISHING

Publishers:
JULES**GAMMOND,** TIM**EXELL,** VANESSA**GARDNER**

Series Editor: VANESSA**GARDNER**

Written by: RALPH**DELLOR and** STEPHEN**LAMB**